Learning from My Mother's Voice

**FAMILY LEGEND
AND
CHINESE AMERICAN IMMIGRATION
EXPERIENCE**

Second Edition – Black/White Version

Jean Lau Chin

DEDICATION

In honor of my mother, Fung Gor Lee.
Dedicated to my parents Kim Lau and Fung Gor Lee,
my husband, Gene S. Chin, my children, Scott and Stephen
and all of my family clan.
In celebration of our bonds
with those before us, those with us, and for those after us.

LEARNING FROM MY MOTHER'S VOICE

CONTENTS

LEARNING FROM MY MOTHER'S VOICE

DETAILED CONTENTS

FOREWORD

The very title of Jean Lau Chin's book—*Learning from My Mother's Voice*—both honors her mother, a courageous woman who immigrated to the United States from China, and indicates her mother's primary role within the text as she describes life both in China and in the United States, as well as her own immigration journey. It is a tribute to her mother and other women who experience immigration then and now.

Examining the life of one's mother often means the exploration of geography (i.e., place), time period, and people central to one's life. It can also mean learning about socialization through literature, particularly mythology and storytelling. In the case of the former, one is limited only by the imagination of the storyteller and the listener. Stories can address racial and/or ethnic geography (see Frankenberg, 1993) and gender geography—that is, the particular people who occupy those physical spaces (see Lightfoot, 1988; Wade-Gayles, 1993; Walker, 1983). In this book, the reader is carried through history and time to varied locations and across several generations through mythology and storytelling that is focused on the lives of Chinese women.

As the reader takes Jean Lau Chin's guided tours through myth and cultural history, it is clear that these stories are more than entertainment. They represent cultural messages about living as a women. The juxtaposition of Chinese and Western myths with their similarities and differences, followed by the author's incisive analysis of contemporary stories depicting Asian women in print and on screen, provide culturally driven connections to perceptions and behaviors of Chinese women both individually and in relation to the world. Through these stories, a rich tapestry of information about Chinese women and Chinese American women emerges. The stereotypical Chinese woman fails to appear as the various lenses of ethnicity, gender, location, and epoch make explicit the diversity that exists within any ethnic group and liberate us by providing an informed array of images and possibilities.

These stories and myths give us context for the voice of Fung Gor Lee, the author's mother. Her autobiography—detailed in a first person narrative in Chapters 4 and 5 of this book—is given additional meaning and when readers are made aware of the literature and myths that shaped not only the perceptions and experiences of Mrs. Lee, but also their own. Here, storytelling takes on new dimensions for the reader and the writer.

Despite daughter and mother living in very different daily worlds, the strong, viable connection maintained between them, as well as their lived stories, confirm that difference does not justify disconnection. Further, telling one's story in cultural context can be a healing experience and an affirmation of worth and value. Through storytelling, mythology, and autobiography, Jean Lau Chin has asserted that her mother's life will continue to matter.

---Jessica Henderson Daniel

References

Frankenberg, R. (1993). *White women, race matters.* Minneapolis, MN: University of Minnesota Press.

Lightfoot, S. L. (1988). *Balm in Gilead.* Reading, MA: Addison-Wesley.

Wade-Gayles, G. (1993). *Pushed back to strength.* Boston, MA: Beacon Press.

Walker, A. (1983). *In search of our mothers' gardens.* New York: Harcourt, Brace & Jovanovich.

INTRODUCTION

Learning from My Mother's Voice celebrates my mother Fung Gor Lee and our mother-daughter relationship. It was first published in 2005 to memorialize my mother ten years after her death—writing the book was a healing exercise for me given her traumatic death after being hit by a car. Now 12 years later--one zodiac cycle and more than 20 years after her death, the first edition is out of print. During this time, I began an Oral History Project and published two volumes about the New York City Chinatown Chinese which profile immigrant families, much like my own, growing up during the 1930s-1960s.(see http://ceoservices.wixsite.com/nycchinatownoralhist). These stories about the immigration experience share themes of bonding and connections, community and psychosocial supports, parental sacrifice, discrimination and resilience to achieve the American dream. More than one decade after the millennium, we see immigration issues, once again front and center in the U.S as plans to erect border walls to keep out the Mexicans, travel bans against Muslims, and deportation of undocumented persons raise tension and fear among immigrant families.

It is time to tell the immigration story once again—of all who came to the US for a better life, made sacrifices so their children could succeed, to achieve the American dream and faced the challenges of poverty and discrimination in that journey. It is time to update write this revision because more than a half century since this story took place, a saga about women, mothers and daughters, and intergenerational bonds are still appealing and timely. While the places, people and sociopolitical contexts have changed, the immigration story remains the same—It is a journey we all make in life.

Storytelling and Legend

Storytelling and sagas have been popular through the ages to capture the meaning and essence of the human condition. Conflict and problem solving, hopes and dreams, losses and trauma, described through legend and myth, have captured and enraptured those through the generations who find commonality with the plight. Storytelling has served as the emotional bridge between storyteller and listener, and provided a therapeutic atmosphere for healing among its listeners. The transformation of the self, accomplished through the use of saga, myth, legend and storytelling has enabled listeners and observers to participate and connect across generations and culture; it has enabled connection with one's roots, and resolution of unsolved life dilemmas. Mythology, fairy tales, and storytelling have captured the imagination and meaning of life for generations—they speak of creation, rebirth, interpersonal and family bonds, and the journey of life. They provide answers to questions about the cycle of life

Each culture has its own set of stories and legends that they cherish and use to sustain and nurture adults and children alike. Immigrant families will develop a saga about their immigration journey which include their dreams, disappointments, and frustrations. These sagas describe the developmental tasks of adapting to a new environment, dealing with daily living, and surviving in an alien culture. They describe the life cycle, beginning with one's creation, progressing to our journey in life, and ending with our transformation of toward enlightenment.

While some see these sagas as universal; others see these differences of culture and generations as serving to exclude and separate us from one another. All immigrants share a dream for a better life. As immigrant families develop these sagas, they create the legends which bond us together—the intergenerational bonds, bonds of creation, bonds between mothers and their sons and daughters, and bonds among families and community; these immigration legends sustain us. But they also can also put us into bondage when our stories of survival and suffering constrain us in our pursuits and isolate us in our enclaves.

The myths and legends rooted in our cultural histories provide the impetus for creating our immigration legends. Nothing captures the journey of Chinese immigration better than *Journey to the West,* a classic 16th century Chinese epic about Monkey King, a smart but rebellious character in his search for enlightenment. As Chinese Americans make their way, Eastern and Western worldviews often are in stark contrast to one another. Classic Chinese legends and myths evolve and are transformed by the passage of time, the influence of Western culture and the juxtaposition of sociopolitical contexts. These immigration legends often derived from opposing worldviews challenge our identities and dichotomize our realities in an illogical bicultural world—but they are central to our forming a positive bicultural identity.

Part I: Mythology and Symbols

Part I of this book is about Chinese mythology and the stories about creation, women, bonds, the cycle of life, and the journey to enlightenment. They are the intergenerational links to the past for Chinese Americans. We see the themes in Chinese mythology mirrored in the life experiences of Chinese American immigrants. The immigrant's journey is compounded by the challenge of being uprooted and transplanted—a theme of creation and rebirth. Psychological themes of separation, abandonment, loss, and guilt often pervade the lives and adjustment of immigrant families despite their different origins and reasons for migration. The journey of immigration is a quest for freedom coupled with losses of family, culture, and homeland.

Chapter 1 focuses on the classic Chinese stories of mythology, moral teachings, and fairy tales that bond us with the past. Many children hear these stories as they are recited to them by parents (as did my mother) or communicated to them through words or deeds. They are shared culture communicating images and messages about women, family, and relationship. They remind us of obligations and the journey we must take in the developmental tasks in life.

Chapter 2 focuses on the contemporary stories that are Chinese American as well as the images about women and Asians in Western stories. It is about biculturalism and the challenges of contrasting Chinese and American cultures and worldviews. It is about transition and adjustment in the evolving image of the Woman Warrior, and of women in a male dominated society. The contrasting images and messages experienced by Chinese American immigrants can oppress and create a lifelong bondage. My mother spent more than 50 years in the United States, but could not speak English and lived within the ½ mile confines of Chinatown. Yet she imparted to us strong Chinese cultural values, pride, and identity. These stories remind us of the fear that we will lose touch with the struggle and striving of our immigrant forebears.

Chapter 3 focuses on the Chinese cultural values found in its symbols. An examination of both contemporary and classical symbols provide the bonds that hold families and communities together. Contrasting Chinese and American cultural symbols also illustrate the challenges that Chinese Americans face in creating their new bicultural identities. Immigrants often cling to the symbols of their culture to retain and restore what was lost. This is through their stories, their food, and their words, and the rituals used sustain the bonds of culture.

Part II: An Intergenerational Saga—Family Legend

Part II is an oral history of my mother and an intergenerational saga about her Journey to the West in immigrating to the United States. The influence of mythology and cultural symbols discussed in Part I plays out in the day to day living within the family and community. The juxtaposition of historical and sociopolitical events between China and the United States during my mother's lifetime sets the context for this saga and enriches the bicultural symbolism and mythology that unfold.

Themes about my mother include her lifelong quest to:

- Fulfill her obligation to family as dictated by her status
- Fulfill her promise to her son who she left at age 5
- Cope with multiple losses, of separation and abandonment,
- Be dutiful through her maternal sacrifice
- Live her life with honor and virtue

A second focus of this saga is the immigration story—a journey of survival and striving, and the trials and tribulations of immigration, racism, acculturation, and poverty which created the bonds and bondage that defined my mother's life. Her maternal sacrifice to husband and family was magnanimous. Her quest to be the good wife and mother was unsurpassed. Though she was constrained by the sociopolitical contexts of women's roles and male dominance, the emergence of communism in China, and the oppression of racism and anti-Chinese immigration in the American culture, her story is one of transformation as she achieved her freedom and was honored and celebrated in her death by all her family, relatives, and friends.

This saga is spoken through the voice of my mother, Fung Gor Lee. The oral history is set in a historical context that spans events of more than a century from the California Gold Rush (1850s to the Japanese invasion of China (1930s), through World War II (1940s), to the political ideologies of communism in China and McCarthyism in the US (1950s), and the Civil Rights and Women's movements (1960s). These events were the trials tests of forbearance faced by many Toisanese immigrants in their journey to the West. Toisanese immigrants from the Guangzhou province of China were the earliest Chinese immigrants, who now make up the fabric of many second and third generation Chinese Americans. The need for cheap labor in the U.S. coupled with the devastating floods in Guangzhou, China fueled the heavy immigration of Chinese men. At the same time, restrictive and discriminatory anti-Chinese legislation heavily influenced patterns of immigration which led husbands to be separated from wives and families for decades.

Part III: Transformation and Enlightenment

Lest future generations lose touch with the immigrant experience of their forebears, Part III is about transformation and the creation of family legend. It is both a process and a journey. It is a process for families to tell their story—their family saga and create their family legend for future generations. It is about revisiting their ancestry through cultural mythology, family saga, and travel. In so doing, it is creates the intergenerational bonds to provide hope for the future and restore faith in the present. The mythology and symbols of our cultures can be both bonds and bondages. The journey is to change the narrative to reduce the bondage that constrain our transformation and expand the bonds that lead us to achieve our enlightenment.

Finally, Chapter 8 is a primer for the lessons to be learned in our images and symbols, messages and words of bonding and bondage. Although this is a saga about one family, all might resonate with the immigration story and the journey we must all take. Although this saga is set in the 20th century, the issues are still relevant to the global economy of the 21st century. Although the instant internet access and rapid travel to the far corners of the world bridge our communities in ways never dreamed possible, the psychological themes of immigration, acculturation, coping with loss, fulfilling obligations, and building character in the journey of life remain constant.

PART I: MYTHOLOGY AND SYMBOLS

We demonstrate how Chinese mythology and cultural legends offering an Eastern worldview are used by Chinese American immigrant families in their daily lives, for survival, and adaptation. All immigrant families draw on their cultural legends as examples for how to conduct themselves socially and morally, and as sources of solace for coping with a hostile host environment, and as comforting reminders of their identity and connections with the culture they left behind. Mythology and cultural legends are statements of difference as well as common bonding. For Chinese women whose history and contributions were often subordinated to men, the legend of the Woman Warrior captures the strength and resiliency of women in male-dominated cultures.

Cultural values are also embodied in our cultural symbols. Given the emphasis within Chinese culture on metaphors and symbolism, images, food and words become the vessels to capture the essence of culture and its values. This traditional Chinese banquet—full of ritual and decorum—best captures the symbols of abundance by the number and quality of dishes, of the generosity of the host, of the harmony and balance in life through the choice of dishes, and of the bonding among the guests in its execution.

Finally, recounting a family saga is often aligned with the sociohistorical saga of a culture and community, each enriching the other. As Chinese American immigrants draw on their cultural legends, and bring them on their journey to the west, they create their family legend for the present and future. World War II, communism in China, and the Civil Rights Movement were some defining events for Chinese immigrants to build their bicultural identities land create their family legends.

CHAPTER 1: MYTHS AND STORYTELLING

Paradise—While the Garden of Eden lies in the East for westerners, the Jade Mountain of the Queen Mother, *Hsi Wang Mu*, lies in the West for Asians. Eve tempted Adam to eat the forbidden apple from the tree of knowledge while Monkey King stole the immortal peach. For this, they were banished from heaven. *Kuan Yin*, the goddess of mercy, took pity on Monkey King, and entreated the Queen Mother to allow Monkey to submit to 81 trials to reach enlightenment. She hovered over him as he journeyed to the west with the Tang monk. Although he could clear thousands of *lei* (miles) in one leap, he had to travel the road by foot for 16 years before he and his companions could transform themselves and reach enlightenment. The different and opposing emphases underlie the contrasting worldviews about women and gender, and about direction in Eastern and Western mythology. Yet, the balance of power between the sexes—male dominance remain similar.

Creation Myths: In the Beginning

According to Genesis (The Holy Bible, 1999, 1:1-2:4), the following is the biblical creation story found in Western culture,

> In the beginning God created the heavens and the earth....God created man in the image of Himself; in the image of God He created them; male and female he created them." The second account from Genesis 1:5-25 says, "God planted a garden of Eden, which is in the east, and there he put the man he had fashioned....You may eat indeed of all the trees in the garden. Nevertheless of the tree of the knowledge of good and evil, you are not to eat, for on the day you eat of it, you shall most surely die....[Not having found a suitable helpmate for man, God] made man fall into a deep sleep. And while he slept, he took one of the ribs and enclosed it in flesh...into a woman, and brought her to the

man".

In contrast, the following is the Chinese creation story, found in many Asian cultures.

> In the beginning of time, all was chaos…Chaos was shaped like a hen's egg. The parts of the egg separated into the Yin and the Yang, the male and female essences of all living things. The lighter parts rose to the top, becoming sky and heaven, while the heavier parts sank to become the earth and sea. The opposing tendencies of male and female are in each of us (Bierlein, 1994, p.53).

All cultures have their creation myths. Our myths found in our literature, fairy tales and stories often provide the lens to our cultures. Read not only for their enjoyment, there themes offer philosophical or psychological viewpoints about the human condition that give meaning to life. They offer symbolic expressions about the rites of passage, such as a metaphoric death of an old and inadequate self toward transformation and rebirth. Two differences between fairy tales and myths, however, are worth emphasizing. Myths generally convey something absolutely unique, often grandiose, and supernatural. Fairy tales, by contrast, are often unusual and improbable but presented as ordinary and every day. A second major difference is that the story endings in myths are nearly always tragic, while always happy in fairy tales. (Bettelheim, 1976, p.37)

Yin and Yang: Gender Roles

The creation myths in Western and Asian cultures gave rise to different images of men and women, and communicate different messages about gender roles. In contrast to the emphasis on male dominance in the Western creation myth of the bible, the Chinese myth emphasizes the duality of gender. It is the opposing tendencies between yin and yang, and the balance between the two that is essential in the universe. Although variations of these themes will be found in all cultures such that we might say there are more commonalities between us than differences, it is the differences that make each individual culture unique and have persisted through the generations.

The relationship between Eve and the serpent in the Bible personifies the exclusion of women from knowledge and power. Eve, or woman, represents the desire, transgression, and shame that Adam, or man, must repress. The God of the West formulates the code of eroticism between the sexes as though it were a code of war; that is, "I will put enmity between thee and woman, and between thy seed and her seed" (Kristeva, 1986, p. 21).

Creation Myth of Immigration: Rebirth

Our histories, it is generally the men who are the warriors and conquerors. They are the pioneers—they built the transcontinental railroad in America. Yet, it is the women, in their role as caretakers, as mothers, and matriarchs, who nurtured and helped to heal from the loss, trauma, and rebirth inherent in the immigration experience. It has been the women who re-created the psychological environment and community networks so comfortable and reminiscent of home. Women's connectedness—as the bearers of children and culture—have been the anchors in Chinese American families. Their acclaim are often unsung—subsumed behind the stature of their men and husbands. These are the stories written by men.

There is a creation myth embedded in the immigration story—one of rebirth as families start afresh. As women retell these stories, we can see that early Chinese American immigrant women toiled along with their men in laundries and restaurants, and performed their unique role of psychological healing and emotional bonding—reinforcing the yin and yang duality of Chinese mythology. Given the scarcity of Chinese women in America at the beginning of the 20th century, they helped to unify and create family in this bachelor husband community through their cooking, caretaking, and healing. They maintained their bonds with family members remaining in China through letter writing which instructed, consoled, and connected. These roles have been largely marginalized as unprofessional and unworthy of acclaim. They were viewed as homemakers, as "not out in the real world" while men were viewed as the breadwinners. Chinese American women contributed to the dual income household by necessity while still defined as helping their husbands in the laundries. They struggled to create a new world, a bicultural one, in the image of the old, for their families here in America.

Myths of Women

In looking at myths through the ages, Bachofen, a Swiss scholar of the Greek classics, came to the conclusion that there were three clear stages in early European culture. The first was a barbaric stage, followed by a matriarchy that in turn, was supplanted by a patriarchy. In the barbaric stage, neither male nor female were dominant in society resulting in widespread sexual promiscuity when children did not know their fathers, women were defenseless, and family life was virtually nonexistent. Aphrodite, the Greek goddess of love, characterized this period.

Next, women banded together for their own defense, leading to the development of a matriarchal society, reflected in the Greek myths of Amazons and fierce woman warriors. The nurturing aspect of female-hood was symbolized by Demeter, goddess of the crops, in the love of the mother and worship of a mother goddess. Revival of these matriarchal themes and images was seen in the TV series aired in 1995 of *Xena*, the warrior princess who combines the two faces of womanhood. She is a savior through her warrior conquests against the best of men. However, unlike most popular male heroes, there is duality in her character of pureness and innocence vs. her dark side given her past evil deeds. But her loyalty and sisterhood to young Gabrielle symbolize the pure, unadulterated innocence of female-hood.

The Greek myth of Oedipus depicts the triangular conflict through three phases of this struggle. Oedipus kills the Sphinx, a symbol of hermaphroditic characteristics. He then marries his mother, ruler of Thebes. Her downfall was interpreted as a transition from matriarchy to patriarchy. Jaspers, a German philosopher, was fascinated by the independent and parallel development of the world's great religions over a comparatively short period in history, roughly five hundred years, during which prophets emerged independently of one another in China, India, Iran, and Europe (Bierlein, 1994, p.300).

Bachofen's theory about this transition to a patriarchal society in European culture has its parallel in Asian culture where according to Kristeva (1986), a matriarchy, derived from peasant customs, preceded the patriarchal Confucian family in China. This revolution in the rules of kinship can be traced to sometime around 1000BC. However, this shift to a patriarchy in China preserved more elements from the earlier matriarchy than its counterpart in European culture. Kristeva hypothesizes that this was due to the extraordinarily advanced development of the matrilineal family in China.

One Chinese myth that mixes history with legend speaks to this image of gender roles during this age. Suffering from the big flood of the Yellow River, Yu the Great (2198 BC) organizes the lands and waters by causing the Yellow River to flow when he opens The Dragon's Gate. According to legend, his creation dance used to tame the waters imitated a feminine form as a symbol of the political authority. When he is caught dancing by his wife, he kills her and turns her to stone, thus representing the sacrifice and fear of the opposite sex to obtain the female's creative power. This legend sets the stage for patrilineal descent; monarchies have since passed from father to son in patriarchal societies.

Veneration for the Mother: Moon Goddesses

Veneration for the mother is found throughout Chinese history in the ideologies of Taoism and Buddhism religions, which opposed itself to Confucianism and fostered many protests to the social order. The Taoist Book of Mountains and Sea tells the story of the Queen Mother of the West, *Hsi Wang Mu*, who lives in a palace on the mythical Jade Mountain in the West. She was originally a monster with a human face, tiger's teeth, and a leopard's tail. But in Taoist legends she became a beautiful goddess, i.e., female, embodying the principle of yin. A peach tree, which blooms only once every three thousand years on the Queen Mother's birthday, grows there; those who eat its fruit gain immortality. It is at her birthday banquet that the legendary character Monkey stole a peach of immortality and was banished from heaven. (Scott, 1980, p.28)

Chinese Buddhism, in turn, has the goddess *Kuan Yin*, whose cult equals and sometimes surpasses that of Buddha himself. *Kuan Yin*, the Goddess of

Mercy, on entering heaven is said to have paused to listen to the cry of the world, as reflected in her name. Kuan Yin has its origins from a 7th century BC story about the daughter of a ruler who refused to marry according to the wishes of her parents, but was determined to enter a nunnery and devote her life to the poor and the sick. (Scott, 1980, p.38) Buddhism and Taoism in a patriarchal Confucian China was often the refuge of women since it acknowledged their equality with men. The difference in precepts between them represent the tension and contrasts between the peasants and nobility, between men and women, and between matriarchy and patriarchy.

In the worship of gods and goddesses, the sun and moon have come to symbolize the essence of male and female respectively. Many cultures believe the moon is a beneficent presence whose light is considered not only favorable, but also indispensable for growth. This contrasts with the sun's power that, in hot countries, seems hostile to life, scorching the earth and destroying living things. The moon is the fertilizing power, and therefore, often believed to cause pregnancy. The moon is changeable and cyclic with its phases and its power to regenerate every month. Its essence, therefore, is female. Like the moon, woman is the life force that ebbs and flows, not only in her nightly and daily rhythm as it does for man, but also in moon cycles and phases. These two changes together produce a rhythm that not unlike the moon and the ocean tides, waxes and wanes, ebbs and flows, so that she is dependent on her inner rhythm. (Harding, 1971, p.65-

66)

The moon goddess, with her fruit as the source for the drink of immortality, is unlike other goddesses; the moon mother has no male god who rules her. Instead, she is the mother of a son to be born again—that is, like Kuan Yin in the East or Virgin Mary in the West. In contrast, the Chinese rely on the lunar calendar and worship the moon goddess or merciful and sacrificing mother while Americans rely on the solar calendar and worship the sun god.

One Ch'ing dynasty novel, *Flowers in the Mirror* (circa 18th century) is both a fantasy and social satire on the plight of women. The author believing in equal opportunity for men and women sets the novel in the reign of Empress Wu who usurped the throne from her son in the early T'ang dynasty (604-705). As punishment for disobeying a decree, Tang Ao is dismissed from his scholarly rank, and forsakes to world for a long journey in search of immortality. Not unlike Gulliver Travels, he passes through many fantastic lands where everything is strange, and comes to the Country of Women where it is the women who are talented and pass the imperial examinations while the men stay at home.

Hua Muk Lan: The Woman Warrior

While these stories speak to the veneration of the mother and the fertilizing power of the moon goddess, they also reinforce the fears of women's power. This power is celebrated in the story of *Hua Muk Lan*, or the Woman Warrior as she is called in the West. One of the most celebrated classics in Chinese culture, *Hua Muk Lan* is the heroine of the Five Dynasties (420-588). Her power lies in her ability to surpass the military skills of men. She is a young woman who loves and reveres her aging father so much that when he is called to battle, she goes in his place disguised as a man since he does not have a son. For 12 years, she distinguishes herself in military battle as a warrior and leads the army to victory. She develops a friendship with a fellow military general whom she later marries after revealing her true self to him. She refuses further promotions, instead returns home to her parents and family to fulfill her obligations to her family.

This Chinese classic focuses on filial piety and contrasts with the theme of triangular conflict, which is celebrated in Western fairy tales such as Snow White and Cinderella. While all three stories are about the journey of an adolescent girl moving toward independence and separation, the conflict in Asian stories is outside the home and emphasizes reunion between parent and child and the absence of intergenerational conflict. In contrast, Western fairy tales focus on mother-daughter conflict where father is the bystander. The developmental task of *Hua Muk Lan* is her replacement of her aging father with the mother is the bystander, in contrast to Western fairy tales that emphasize the adolescent girl's beauty as competitive and threatening to the mother figure. Western fairy tales focus on the theme of sexual maturity and the mother figure as a formidable opponent, In the Asian fairy tale, the parents are not in conflict with the child's ascendance; *Hua Muk Lan* chooses to leave home, and to fulfill her responsibility and obligation to the family as the oldest sibling. In Western fairy tales, the female is passive and receptive; Snow White and Cinderella both need to be rescued by the charming prince.

Heroines of Strength and Power

The story of *Hua Muk Lan* persists in popularity among the Chinese who love her intelligence, cleverness, and responsibility to the family. However, her journey, transformation, and military excellence or power can be achieved only if she ceases to live as a woman. She is celebrated particularly because this warrior image is at odds with the subordinate roles of woman during Confucian China.

Despite the veneration for the mother in the East, the plight of women was oppressive under Confucian and feudal society in China as it was in America. A frequent theme is that of the worthy Chinese woman, who braves death by letting herself be killed without flinching before the enemy or by committing suicide to facilitate the patriotic or revolutionary task of her husband or her clan. This theme is illustrated in *The Guwen*, a collection of classical texts. (Kristeva, 1986, p.94) The heroine martyr is often celebrated in Chinese history is one who commits suicide as a means for rebellion among young females. Having committed themselves to far reaching ideals of emancipation in communist China, they found no concrete means of realizing them such that Mao Tse Tung wrote, "He who commits suicide is not motivated by a desire for death...it is the most emphatic demonstration of the will to live—an emphasis on how societies can seized their hopes and brutally crushed them."(Kristeva, 1986, p.110)

In 20th century China, the bourgeois revolution of 1912 and the May 4th Movement of 1919 were significant moments of the Women's Movement because they threatened the Chinese family's patriarchy (Kristeva, 1986, p. 97; Barlow & Bjorge, 1989). Despite the favoritism toward males throughout Chinese history, there are exemplars of women who transcended their roles to validate the strength of women. One such woman was Ding Ling, one of China's most colorful and important women writers of the early 20th century. She wrote about women and their emotions during a time when this was taboo. She also wrote of their plight and strivings to be seen as intellectual equals with men. She collided with the Communist Party, and was imprisoned by the Nationalists during the Cultural Revolution, well before the feminist movement in the West. Chinese American women are often perceived to be "behind Western women" in the women's movement when, in fact, the height of these intellectual and political movements in China occurred well before its zenith in America.

These classic stories have an appeal because they speak to our psyche and the developmental tasks of life. As these stories evolve over time, across contexts, and between cultures, they speak to how gender roles have evolved as we have seen in the revival of classic Western fairy tales such as *Beauty and the Beast* by Disney. Similarly, *Hua Muk Lan* was rewritten as a contemporary story in *The Woman Warrior* (Kingston, 1989), and *Mulan,* an animated Disney film about Chinese American women.

Male-Female and Family Bonds

The relationship between men and women is also captured in myths and symbols. Symbols of women merge the images of mother and wife, while those of men merge the images of father and son. In Asian culture, male and female symbols are interdependent—as in a yin-yang balance of the universe. These serve to describe and prescribe gender roles

Sun and Moon Myths: Battle of the Sexes

The popular sun myth in Chinese culture is connected with the last of the Five Emperors, Yao, who was in danger of losing his throne. According to the story, there were ten suns who lived in the Valley of Light. At one point, all ten suns appeared in the sky at once and everything on earth was in danger of being burned. Emperor Yao gave a magic bow to Yi, the Divine Archer, who shot down nine of the suns, leaving only one. The sun is made of fire and symbolizes, the male principle yang. However, the divine archer had a wife, Ch'ang-O, who stole from him the herb of immortality, given to him by the Queen Mother of the West.(Scott, 1980, p.30). As punishment, she was banished to the moon.

Women shine in the reflection of their husbands in this image, not unlike the relationship between the sun and the moon. In Confucian Chinese literature, women were often portrayed as seducers, whose rise to power was often indirect or shameless. These stories about women often spoke of their beauty; their virtues including their unselfish loyalty and devotion to their husbands (Yu, 1974a; 1974b; Kristeva, 1986, p.87). Unlike

Hua Muk Lan, women in these stories more often achieved their power as concubines or courtesans since this was typically their only access to positions of power during feudal times. One of these famous concubines frees herself from her role as servant to become empress, *Wu Zetian*. She accomplishes this by accusing the then empress of killing her child, whom in fact she has killed herself. Her rule is characterized by her independent and even fearsome lifestyle. She undercuts the influence of the ruling class, given her Buddhist origins, by instituting the system of competitive examinations for civil servants.

Many stories of Chinese heroines combine history and legend and were often women of great character with stories of sacrifice and determination as they tried to fulfill their conflicting responsibilities. (Yu, 1974, p.2) They typically achieve power and fame through their cleverness, responsibility, or prowess; in the end, they reunite with their families of origin as the final test of maturity.

Mother and Son Bonds

Male-female relationships in Asian culture are also portrayed in stories about mother-son bonds. While the journey of separation-individuation or independence from parents is a major theme, the importance of a son's loyalty and obligation to the family is also stressed. Many Chinese myths and stories emphasize the importance of the bond between mother and son while Western stories emphasize the triangular conflict of a couple against an interfering mother-in-law. The figure of the mother in Chinese stories is often benevolent and supportive.

Several stories in classic Chinese literature stand out because they speak to a mother's influence on her son, and are frequently recited by mothers to their children. While the father of Confucius is generally unknown, his mother plays an important role as his protector and inspiration. *Yueh Fei*, was a famous patriot and military leader of the Sung dynasty. His mother, Yau, is famous because the Chinese believe his virtue of bravery and loyalty to China came from his mother's lessons, and from the 4 words she tattooed on his back, "Be patriotic to the country". The development of Mencius, a famous Chinese philosopher, was greatly attributed to the influence of his mother who moved three times to ensure that they lived in an environment conducive to development of his character, the last being next to a school where he imitated the scholars. These stories were adapted in the contemporary Asian American novel, *The Woman Warrior* (Kingston, 1989).

Oedipus and Ajase Complex: Triangular Conflict

In Western culture and literature, the Oedipus complex, which emphasizes male development and the paternal-son bond, stands in stark contrast to the Ajase complex within Asian culture, which emphasizes the mother-son bond. The contrasts between these two myths define common universal themes. Similarly, in both tales, the unlikely hero, the boy or the son, proves himself through slaying dragons, solving riddles, and living by his wits and goodness.

Here is the story of Oedipus: Terrified by the prophecy that his child would murder his father and marry his mother, Laius the king of Thebes withdraws from his wife. In complicity to conceive a son, she gets him drunk and seduces him. Laius pierces the baby boy's feet and leaves it to die. The baby is rescued by a shepherd who names the child Oedipus, meaning swollen foot. He is presented to King Polybus, and later becomes heir. In seeking advice about who his parents are, he is told of the oracle. Shocked, he leaves their court.

On the road out of the city, he encounters King Laius, his biological father. In the confrontation as to who should pass first, Oedipus kills his father. He meets up with the Sphinx, who terrorizes Thebans by refusing passage to those who cannot answer its riddles. Oedipus answers the riddle, thereby freeing the Thebans of its domination. Oedipus becomes king and unknowingly marries Jocasta, his mother. A plague falls on Thebes because this violation of the basic laws of gods could not go unpunished. In trying to rid Thebes of the plague, Oedipus finds out his true origins. Queen Jocasta hangs herself. Oedipus, seized with remorse and disgust, gouges out his own eyes, and takes to wandering the earth.

In contrast to the Oedipus complex where a boy has murderous wishes against his father and erotic desires for his mother, the Asian Ajase complex, based on an Indian myth, emphasizes the intensity of the mother and son relationship. Prince Ajase, who was destined to kill his father, becomes king, as does Oedipus. He later tries to kill his mother because she is loyal to his father, the dead king. However, Ajase feels too guilty and cannot accomplish this. As punishment for his transgressions, sores develop on his body, and an odor emanates from them that is so offensive, no one will come near. His mother is the only person willing to care for him. King Ajase's heart responds to his mother's display of affection and forgiveness; thus, he and his mother are reunited. (Okonogu, 1980, quoted by Tatara, 1980, in Chin et al, 1993).

Balance of Power between the Sexes

As these myths of mother and sons, and husbands and wives suggest, the mother or wife takes the active role in both Asian and Western mythology. As wife, in both Asian and Western mythology, she is the temptress whose rise to power is shameless or complicit. As mother in Asian mythology, she is powerful, benevolent, forgiving, nurturing, and a mentor. This contrasts with Western mythology where she is weak or wicked.

As we translate these stories into the lives of Chinese American immigrant families, the celebration of female strengths is subordinated to male dominance in both American and Chinese societies. Female strengths remain covert, because their implied threat to male power is destructive. Yet, male competition and aggressiveness is overt.

Family and Generational Bonds

The family unit is of great importance in Chinese culture, and is defined to include the extended family. While family is important in most cultures, the emphasis on loyalty and obligation to the family in Chinese culture with its origins in Confucianism supersedes the emphasis on the individual in Western culture.

Confucianism and Taoism: Male Dominance vs. Equality

Prior to the establishment of the Republic of China, Chinese families followed the Confucian tradition, which prescribed a hierarchical order of relationships stressing the importance of filial piety and ancestral worship. It is these characteristics that is are most commonly known in the West as "Chinese culture". In an agrarian society, the passage of land from father to son and the need for physical labor was essential to the survival of the family. The family was essentially an economic unit in which males were dominant. Confucianism ensured this continuity by stressing the son's reverence for his father and his role as the heir apparent to the ancestral line.

Submissiveness to authority of the family and government was emphasized. Women and children were subordinate to men. Males were esteemed and valued. They were given the privilege of having multiple wives, as a demonstration of their wealth and social status. The only true mother was the first wife; all others were considered concubines with greater value if they produced sons. In order to enhance the power of the family, the children of all the wives belonged to the first wife or Dai Ma (Eldest mother). The power in the family rested with the father, eldest son, and grandmother or eldest mother. (Kristeva, 1986, p.80)

Confucianism resulted in the increasing importance of the father-son relationships, dictated more by economic reasons, unlike the emotional bonds emphasized in mother-son relationships. Familiarity between father and daughter was more permissible, different from the distance, formality and severity that was expected between father and son. While this gave women more latitude in their behavior, it also meant a total disregard of females in a social order where males reigned as the ancestors to be worshipped. Under Confucianism, women were destined only for housework and reproduction. The words of several Confucian scholars suggest the need to suppress the strivings of women. Yang Chen of the Han dynasty says, "If women are given work that requires contact with the outside, they will sow disorder and confusion throughout the Empire." Sima Guang of the Song dynasty says, "Give a woman an education and all you will get from her is boredom and complaints." (Kristeva, 1986, p.76)

Confucianism pervaded Chinese American society during the early wave of Toisanese immigrants to the United States; most Chinese immigrants were well versed in classic Confucian teachings transmitted through storytelling or reading of the classics, and behaved in accordance with its principles. Most important were the principles of filial piety illustrated by the *Twenty-Four Stories of Filial Piety* (see Tseng & Hsu, 1972); these classic stories prescribed moral principles for the relationship between generations, extolling the virtues of industriousness, respect for one's parents, and obligation to the family. They have been influential in Chinese childrearing analogous to the childrearing books of Dr. Benjamin Spock.

The Taoist and Buddhist religions, on the other hand, has never ceased to fight the Confucian paternalistic hierarchy. Women in China embraced Taoism as a religion because it emphasized the equality of women with men. Westerners often fail to realize this ambivalence within the Chinese psyche, and the parallel challenge to Confucianisn.

Triumph of the Elders: Intergenerational Bonds

In Chinese folklore and stories, defiance of parental authority results in the admonition, punishment, or death of the transgressor (i.e., the children). If the child survives, he/she is often given opportunity for training and atonement. In conflicts between generations, the elders always triumph (Tseng & Hsu, 1972, pp.28-34). Many of the Twenty-Four Stories deal with how the son obtains food for his mother. In five of these stories, the mother is sick and special food is required for her recovery. The stories

also emphasize that if is ideal for families to maintain continuity without conflict between generations.   The parent is expected to protect the child while the child is expected to return this kindness in adulthood, showing mutual interdependence between generations.

The powerfulness of parental authority is presented in another classic Chinese story of a young couple in love against the wishes of their parents; they are unsuccessful in their defiance, and are united only in their death when they transform into a pair of butterflies.

These stories contrast with Western fairy tales such as Hansel and Gretel, whose parents are poor and worry about how to take care of their children. In this tale, the children decide to leave home together because they fear that their parents are plotting to desert them and starve them to death. The experience of mother abandonment is paramount here, which is opposed to the Asian theme of maternal protection and benevolence. Their journey takes them to the gingerbread house of the witch or bad mother.   The witch's evil design forces the children to recognize the dangers of unrestrained oral greed and dependence. In relying on ego and intelligent assessment, they are able to trick the witch into climbing into the oven, thereby freeing them (Bettelheim, 1976).

We see among contemporary Chinese American families ways in which the eldest son was favored unconditionally. This also meant that the older brother had an obligation to protect and be responsible for his sisters. This often took its toll on the normal, carefree urges of childhood among male children.

The Journey: Transformation

As we journey through life, we often strive to reach a state of enlightenment. As Chinese immigrant families journey to the west, they similarly are in a quest for freedom and enlightenment.

Interdependence and Reunification

The developmental task of achieving adulthood is portrayed in many stories of sisterhood and brotherhood; these are stories of self-actualization, identity, transformation, and enlightenment. In *Grimm's Fairy Tales* of Western culture, brother and sister themes often feature the adventures of two siblings representing disparate natures of the self which must be integrated for human happiness. Transformations to an animal existence represent impulse and instinctual desires, while reversion back to human form denotes achieving maturity. This transformation requires a journey and leaving the orbit of the home. One such Grimm fairy tale "Brother and Sister" begins with a lack of differentiation between two siblings, whose wanderings lead them to a spring. Brother gives in to his instinctual desires, and after drinking from the spring turns into a fawn. Sister vows never to leave her brother and protects him until he returns to his human form. Both go through several transformations before achieving maturity. (Bettelheim, 1976, p.91)

Variation to this theme involve Two Brothers symbolizing incompatible aspects of the human personality, not unlike the splitting of the good and bad in the bible story of Cain and Abel. Common to these stories is how two heroes, one of whom is cautious and reasonable, is ready to risk his life to rescue the other brother who foolishly exposes himself to terrible perils. While Western literature often highlights the theme of sibling rivalry, as in Cain and Abel, Chinese literature often emphasizes the importance of interdependence and teamwork. The fairy tale of *Seven Brothers* involves loyal brothers set out to please their father. The Emperor set a heavy tax on the land made rich by the brothers. The brothers embark on a journey to reason with the Emperor to protect their land and their father. They meet with resistance, and it is only by teaming together with their different supernatural assets that they are able to overcome the Emperor--"Together we stand invincible" (Chang, 1968, p.64).

Romance of the Three Kingdoms: Chivalry and Obligation

Romance of The Three Kingdoms is one of the great Chinese classics, a literary masterpiece written by Luo Guanzhong in the 13th century. It begins during the Ming dynasty and ends in the founding of the Chin dynasty (AD 265-420) during the golden age of chivalry in Chinese history. The semi-fictional novel includes tales of military exploit as brothers contest for the throne, and kingdoms are conquered.

After the last of the Han Emperors was assassinated, China was divided into three feudal kingdoms. The end of the Han Dynasty is one of the most turbulent periods in China's history where corruption was rampant in the imperial court. Coupled with natural disasters such as floods, plague and locust swarms devouring the crops, hunger and dissatisfaction among the peasants escalated until the Yellow Scarves Rebellion, led by Zhang Jiao, broke out (so named because the rebels tied yellow scarves on their heads). Unable to put down the rebellion with the government troops, Emperor Ling issued a call to warlords across the country for assistance in suppressing the rebellion. This resulted in a struggle for power among the warlords rendering the Han Emperor powerless.

Out of this struggle in the early 220s A.D. emerged the sovereignty of three smaller states: Wei, Wu and Shu. Historians debate over which of these three kingdoms was the legitimate heir to the Han Dynasty although they now generally recognize the Wei Kingdom created by Cao Cao as the official imperial line or Mandate of Heaven (see http://www.3kingdoms.net/intro.htm.

The tales of courage and adventure in this classic literary masterpiece of more than 1,700 years ago are still popular among the Chinese today; the heroes—Liu Bei, Cao Cao, Kuan Yu, Zhang Fei, and Zhuge Liang—are household names. *Romance of the Three Kingdoms* is not only about the struggle and conflicts among the warlords; it is also about loyalty, betrayal, courage, lust, determination, responsibilities, repaying the kindness of others and trust among brothers; it is about chivalry and obligation to serve one's country within the Chinese culture.

The stories are used as examples of brotherhood, loyalty, and obligation as three brothers fight for the throne—values that guide behavior in Chinese American immigrant families. The mother-son bond between Liu Bei and his mother is reiterated as a virtue. Male aggression is celebrated through the cunning of military strategy and adventures of the military campaigns; the transformation of the hero is in his leadership and reinforces Confucian values and principles. There is much symbolism in the animal names of the generals whose characteristics reflect their leadership styles. The peach orchard in which the oath was sworn is the symbol of immortality.

Books have been written about Chinese military strategy from this period, and are used to understand characteristics of modern leadership. The heroes of this classic are often studied for their character traits as they contribute to effective leadership styles. Thus, this classical novel remains popular because it illustrates the journey taken by its heroes, and provides insight into human character and the human condition within Chinese culture. It is comparable to discussing the impact of the Revolutionary War in America.

Journey to the West vs. Star Wars: Transformation

Journey to the West and Star Wars are two sagas illustrating some contrasting differences between Asian and Western cultures respectively. While they are stories of adventure, underlying themes speak to transformation of character. Journey to the West, a 16th century epic written by Wu Ch'eng, is a renowned classical Chinese novel about an allegorical rendition of a journey in search of the scriptures; it is mingled with Chinese fables, fairy tables, legends, and demon adventures with origins in the Taoist and Buddhist religions. It was based on a true story of a famous Chinese monk, Xuan Zang (602-664) in the 5th century AD. After years of traveling on foot to what is now India, the birthplace of Buddhism, to seek the *Sutra*, the Buddhist holy book, he goes through trials and tribulations. After returning to China, or Tang Mountain (Tang San) as China was called at that time, with the *sutra*, his translation of them into Chinese contributes greatly to the development of Buddhism in China.

Journey to the West is divided into three parts: 1) an early history of the Monkey spirit; 2) pseudo-historical account of Hsuan-Tsang's family and life before his trip to fetch the *sutra* in the Western Heaven; and 3) the main story, consisting of 81 dangers and calamities encountered by Hsuan Tsang and his three animal spirit disciples.

Three disciples join Hsuan-Tsang on his quest for the Buddhist scriptures from the Queen Mother of the West—the clever, acrobatic and impudent Monkey, the gluttonous Pig, and the river spirit, Sha Monk, representing mind, body, and spirit, respectively. The team travels for 16 years, encountering adventures with supernatural and mythic beings, and fight fearsome battles with demons and spirits, all the while guided by the compassionate goddess, Kuan Yin. The external adventures are colorful, action oriented, and full of fantasy; the four travelers need to learn to distinguish truth from fiction, demons from spirits, and avoid being fooled by appearances. These external adventures are paralleled by inward explorations of the human psyche within each of the characters who become enlightened and achieve a transformation in the process of this journey.

Journey to the West is not unlike the popular Western epic Star Wars, termed a "modern developmental fairy tale" by McDermott and Lum (1980). *Star Wars* takes place in another galaxy in a future time. It is a trilogy of adventure that center around three characters—Luke Skywalker, Han Solo, and Princess Leia—who are forced to band together by circumstance rather than friendship. At the beginning, Princess Leia, a leader of the Rebel Alliance, is captured and taken aboard the evil Galactic Empire's mobile command station, the impregnable Death Star. Prior to her capture, she entrusted the plans to destroy the Death Star to R2D2, the little robot, hoping he and his caretaker, C3PO, also a robot, can reach a former general of the Old Republic, Obi-Wan Kenobi. The pair end up becoming farm hands for the uncle of Luke Skywalker. After Luke's uncle and aunt are killed, the three embark on their adventure to save the planet. They engage Han Solo, a mercenary pilot, to rescue Princess Leia. Despite great odds and many adventures, the trio with the help of "The Force" is able to destroy the Death Star and restore the Republic. This saga has many things in common with *Journey to the West*: the elements of fantasy, supernatural powers, good vs. evil, and action. The trio also goes through transformation and travel under the support of "the Force.

There are significant contrasts between the two sagas that distinguish their cultural origins. In *Journey to the West*, the parents are symbolically represented by female authority figures—the spiritual and supreme beings of Kuan Yin and Hsi Wang Mu are spiritual and supreme beings, who watch over the travelers. In *Star Wars*, the parent is represented by male authority figure Obi Wan Kenobi, who watches over the trio; and by Darth Vader, another male authority figure who thwarts, threatens, and almost destroys the trio. These two represent two opposing sides of a powerful force. The need to destroy the parental authority figures in Western mythology as the hero goes through his transformation and maturation is what distinguishes it from Asian mythology, where the benevolent authority figure remains intact.

Both Monkey King and Luke Skywalker long for adventure and are impatient.; their transformation is analogous to adolescent maturation while the Tang monk is more adult maturation. In *Journey to the West*, components of self are embodied in Monkey, Pig, and River Spirit, that is, impulse, bodily desire, and spirit; the developmental task is in their moderation and containment. In *Star Wars*, Luke's idealism is pitted against Han Solo's cynicism, selfishness, and sense of omnipotence; the developmental task is in his self-expression.

Repressed images of childhood are depicted in both sagas. The barroom (cantina) in *Star Wars* is like a frontier saloon and embodies visual evidence of evil and ugliness, representing the present corrupt world. In *Journey to the West*, the seduction by the material world is represented in the substory of Seven Spider Spirits. The Tang monk is lured into Gossamer Cave by seven spider spirits disguised as beautiful women. His rescue by Monkey and Pig emphasize the importance of interdependence and teamwork.

The fight between good and evil is a spiritual one in the story of Monkey King. Monkey King fights demon spirits while Luke Skywalker fights the evil Empire. In *Star Wars*, the ultimate fight is between father and son as Luke Skywalker discovers that Darth Vader of the evil Empire is his father. The journey to adulthood is played out differently once again; the son must be victorious over the powerful father figure in Western literature. By contrast, the emphasis in Asian literature is in the transformation of Monkey King with the result that he is granted forgiveness and immortality by the Queen Mother, His Wang Mu.

The journey for each is also different. Han Solo and Luke Skywalker are out to destroy the evil forces; they succeed because the vulnerability of Death Star was in its designer's inability to conceive of the fact that one small space ship could be a threat to it—symbolizing the failing of the father to see the threat of the son. By contrast, Monkey King, must subdue his impulsive and temperamental tendencies to achieve enlightenment, represented by the crown, which gives him headaches whenever he has bad thoughts. The rebelliousness and cunning of Monkey is internal and must be contained in order to succeed over the demons and spirits outside.

These differences reflect different worldviews of man against nature. In the Asian culture, man must establish harmony with nature while in Western culture, man must overcome it. Both epics are appealing because they tap into the meaning of life, self-identity and value systems, separation and individuation; achievement of maturity; and overcoming of problems of dependency, abandonment, and death.

Journey to the West: Chinese Immigration

Journey to the West is an allegory for the journey of immigration. Many will agree that Monkey King, who is full of cunning, prowess, and wisdom, is also an allegory for the rebellious spirit against the then untouchable feudal rulers in China. His plight is not unlike the trials and challenges all Chinese American immigrants face before achieving enlightenment. Monkey King is punished for hundreds of years, but remains rebellious and formidable against his parental figures. His transformation is not unlike that of Chinese American immigrants in fighting discrimination and creating a bicultural identity.

Monkey King: Clever and Rebellious

An examination of the beloved character Monkey King is important to capture the psyche and transformation process of Chinese American immigrants (see http://www.china-on-site.com/pages/comic/comiccatalog1.php). Monkey King is a rebellious and extraordinary being, born out of a rock, fertilized by the grace of Heaven. Being extremely smart and mischievous, he learned all the magic tricks and kung fu from a master Taoist; he was able to transform himself into seventy-two different images such as a tree, a bird, a beast of prey or a bug as small as a mosquito to sneak into an enemy's belly to fight him inside.

Using clouds as a vehicle, he can travel 180,000 li (miles) in a single somersault; he carried a huge iron bar that could expand or shrink at his command as his favorite weapon in his feats. He claimed to be king in defiance of the authority and Supreme Being—the Great Jade Emperor. That act of treason coupled with complaints from the masters of the four seas and hell invited the relentless scourge of the heavenly army. After many showdowns, the emperor, unable to defeat him, had to offer the monkey an official title to appease him. Enraged when he learns that the position he held was nothing but that of a stable keeper, he revolts, fighting his way back to earth to resume his own claim as a king.

Eventually, the heavenly army subdued him, only after many a battle, with the help of all the god warriors. Because he has a bronze head and iron shoulders, all methods of execution failed and the monkey dulls many a sword inflicted upon him. As a last resort, the emperor commanded that he be burned in the furnace where his Taoist minister, Tai Shang Lao Jun refines his pills of immortality. Instead of killing him, the fire and smoke adds to Monkey King a pair of fiery golden crystal eyes that can see through what people normally cannot. He fought his way down again. Finally, under Buddha's help, the monkey is suppressed under a great mountain known as the Mount of Five Fingers and he could not move. Five hundred years later, he is rescued by the Tang monk, Hsuan Tsang, and becomes his disciple on the journey to the west.

Eighty-One Trials to Enlightenment

In *Journey to the West*, the goddesses and parental authority put the Tang monk and his three disciples through 81 tests before they can obtain the scriptures and reach enlightenment. The number 81 is a multiple of 9 x 9 with nine symbolizing longevity or immortality; the struggle is transcendence to another level of consciousness or heaven in Western terms. As Monkey so aptly puts it, he can leap a thousand li (i.e., miles) to get to where he wants in a second, but he must accompany the Tang monk on foot to reach his destiny in 16 years; the developmental process cannot be rushed. Similarly the number 16 is a multiple of 4 x 4 with four symbolizing death.

Luke and Han Solo, on the other hand, are fighting an intergalactic war (i.e., in this world) against powerful parental figures who wish to control the world and destroy them. The character of Princess Leia clearly breaks with tradition from the helpless and seductive female now more common in contemporary literature.

Monkey King is analogous with Adam in their original sin. While both violate the wishes of the paternal figure, Adam is tempted by a female figure while Monkey King is protected by the maternal figure. While both are banished from heaven, Adam's original sin is the root of human suffering. Monkey King, on the other hand, is punished for hundreds of years, but remains rebellious and formidable against the Emperor—paternal figure. He is rescued by the Tang monk (benevolent father symbol) and protected by Kuan Yin (nurturing maternal symbol); in his journey, he can atone and gain forgiveness, enabling him to return to heaven.

Journey of Immigration

The early Toisanese Chinese immigrants were known for their rebellious seafaring spirit. Their suffering, rendered by the floods wreaking havoc on the crops and causing massive starvation forced the immigration in search of the Golden Mountain of the West, (i.e., San Francisco Gold Rush). During their journey, they faced major trials and challenges, including having to fight against the racist policies of anti-Asian sentiment and legislation. Monkey's fight against the heavenly army is not unlike the immigration experience.

The character of Monkey King is not unlike the unbreakable spirit of the early Chinese American immigrants, who were also described as cunning and devious, for their tendency to be "inscrutable". These negative portrayals are transcended because Monkey King is loved by the Chinese for his smart (cunning) and spirited (rebellious) character. The rebelliousness of Chinese immigrants against the unjust and racist policies of the U.S led many to defy the rules in their years of illegal immigration to the U.S..

CHAPTER 2: CONTEMPORARY STORYTELLING AND IMMIGRATION LEGEND

The Creation of Legend: Warrior Images

Storytelling continues throughout the ages. Those that capture our imagination and provide us answers about the cycle of life persist and create the legends that sustain us. *Stars Wars* (Lucas, 1977), *Crouching Tiger, Hidden Dragon* (Lee, 2004), and *The Woman Warrior* (Kingston, 1989) are several such stories that feature women in warrior roles. Cast in contemporary, spiritual, fantasy and futuristic contexts, these stories of adventure, journey and transformation continue to draw on cultural images, themes, and values of the past while they have evolved to our global and diverse contemporary society.

Crouching Tiger, Hidden Dragon: Identity Transformation

Ang Lee's movie, *Crouching Tiger, Hidden Dragon,* is a contemporary movie set in the 19th century that creates legend and myth based on Chinese culture. Its popularity and impact lies in how it impresses the power of myth upon those of us who thought it lost (Simpson, 2001). Unlike classic Asian myths, the main protagonists are female. Yet like many Asian classics, it concludes with the death of the main protagonists, the lovers' union ending in tragic suicide, and the benevolence of the symbolic mother.

According to Campbell (1949), several

characters in myths are constants; hero, mentor, shadow, and the trickster. The hero's journey typically results in his/her transformation—the eternal struggle for identity in Western myths or enlightenment in Eastern myths. Such stories are appealing because we are each on a similar journey in real life. Adapting a 1930s Chinese novel by Wang Du Lu, Ang Lee crafted a "dream of China" where the everyday merges with the fantastical by using a common format in Chinese martial arts movies. However, *Crouching Tiger, Hidden Dragon* is different from the classical hero's journey that is typically male and analogous as a rite of passage; in this movie, Ang Lee creates a feminine tale of self-discovery. Therefore, it is both classic and feminist.

Shu Lien, the heroine, arrives in Beijing and observes two young girls entertaining on the street. She is disdainful because she views these girls as slaves; yet, she too is trapped by her fate to remain a warrior. She envies the "freedom" of the princess Jen to be the feminine Asian female.

In the movie, the ancient sword of legendary warrior, Li Mu Bai, (the male mentor) is stolen. In seeking enlightenment, he gave up his sword and entrusted it to his female warrior ally, Shu Lien, to take it to Governor Yu in Beijing for safekeeping. The sword is stolen by the trickster princess Jen, and protected by Jade Fox, the shadowy nemesis who killed Li Mu Bai's mentor. Li M Bai is forced to become a warrior again in order to avenge his mentor's death.

Both Li Mu Bai and Jade Fox want Jen as their disciple, but are deceived by her—an intergenerational theme. Li Mu Bau and Li Shen represent the good parental figures who remain true to their virtues and character, clearly an Asian theme; both suppress their feelings toward one another during their many years together as warrior allies. Li Shen does not marry or fulfill her love for Li Mu Bai out of loyalty to his brother to whom she was engaged, an Asian female virtue but a bondage of cultural values.

Li Mu Bai embodies the characteristics of both the Crouching Tiger, Hidden Dragon. He demonstrates his warrior prowess in his masterful use of martial arts—a characteristic of the tiger. When he comes in touch with his affectionate feelings for Li Shen, he plans to give up the sword in his quest for enlightenment--a characteristic of the dragon. In Western culture, this quest is an embodiment of his "feminine side" or emotional side while in Asian culture, it is the juxtaposition of both male and female characteristics. (Simpson, 2001). Both Li Mu Bai he and Li Shen are trapped by their past. as warriors; they are the good but powerful parental figures--martial arts masters unbeatable in their battle for justice, but benevolent in their treatment of Jen.

Unknown to them, Jen has superior hidden martial arts skills, learned from the manual stolen by Jade Fox from the Wudan Academy to which Li Mu Bau belonged. The spectacular martial arts feats performed by the protagonists are legendary in Chinese classics. Green Destiny, Li Mu Bai's sword has obvious parallels to the Western legendary sword Excalibur of King Arthur. The rooftop chase between Jen and Li Mu Bai mirrors thos of the classic Arabian Nights.

The flashback encounter between the young lovers, Jen and Lo (she is the dragon and he is the tiger) in the Gobi desert is free and impulsive, in contrast with that of the older lovers, which is contained and suppressed. Jen is an upstart aristocrat who goes through various transformations of spoiled brat, errant thief, hearty fighter, and passionate lover. She is the trickster and heroine, her admirable qualities conflicting with her darker side and impulses. The full extent of her powers is revealed in the bar fight and observed by Li Mui Bai and Shu Lien. Li Mui Bai wants to mentor her believing he could trust that her purer qualities will prevail. She makes a formidable opponent and while both Li Mu Bai and Shu Lien end up in combat with Jen, neither have the heart to kill her despite the opportunity and her betrayal.

Symbolism and Character Development

Crouching Tiger Hidden Dragon taps deeply into ancient Chinese myths. Criticisms cited by Simpson about the movie being "nothing more than a bag of tricks" reflect a failure of many Westerners to understand the symbolism and values of Asian culture. Angered at Jen's betrayal (she steals the martial arts secrets by exploiting Jade Fox's inability to read the stolen book), Jade Fox attempts to poison Jen. In attempting to rescue her, Li Mui Bai is himself poisoned by Jade Fox. Jen is too late in her attempts to find an antidote. The movie ends with Jen, the young female trickster, taking a leap of faith as a reward for becoming a "pure warrior"; the ending is ambiguous as to whether this is suicide (a common ending in Asian classics) to atone for her guilt over being responsible for Li Mui Bai's death.

Crouching Tiger Hidden Dragon is a movie rich in symbolism. The dragon in Chinese myth and legend is a beneficent figure, blessed, and chief of all the reptiles with powers of transformation—Li Mui Bai's transformation is internal; Jen's is external. In Christian mythology, by contrast, the dragon is a symbol of sin and evil.. It is often represented It is often represented as crushed under the feet of saints and martyrs, symbolizing the triumph of Christianity over paganism. The Chinese dragon symbolizes power and excellence, valiancy and boldness, heroism and perseverance, nobility and divinity. A dragon overcomes obstacles until success is his. He is energetic, decisive, optimistic, intelligent and ambitious. The dragon confers the essence of life, in the form of its sheng chi (celestial breath), and bestows its power in the form of the seasons, bringing water from rain, warmth from the sunshine, wind from the seas and soil from the earth. The dragon is the ultimate representation of the forces of mother nature, the greatest divine force on Earth.

These dragon characteristics of Jen are hidden when she is behaving as the aristocratic princess; which is shown by her impatience to reveal her hidden self and power. This story is both atypical and contemporary in its portrayal of male and female characteristics, given that it features women warriors with dragon characteristics—Li Shen. At the same time, it is classic in that women needed to disguise themselves if they are to be warriors--Jen. The identity struggle is contemporary because the protagonists' search for enlightenment is a journey that mirrors the transformation process of Chinese American immigrants.

The contemporary Woman Warrior: Paradoxes

The *Woman Warrior: Memoirs of a Girlhood among Ghosts,* by Maxine Hong Kingston (1989), is a contemporary novel of an American-born daughter of Chinese immigrant parents. It illustrates the paradoxical nature of the Chinese American experience through the eyes of an American born Chinese using family history, "talk-story", memory, legend, and imaginative projection. Speaking from two vantage points, the narrator sees double almost all the time. Secrets are never said in front of the *bak gwai* (white demons or Americans); culture is lived and not explained. These practices are confusing and nonsensical unless understood within a cultural context. Although the novel alludes to the many nuances characteristic of Chinese American immigrant families, critics have challenges the author's distortion of Chinese legends. Kingston argues that is not a chronicle of history, but a novel, and records the legends as it is remembered.

One of the most critical contradictions facing the Chinese American woman character in *The Woman Warrior* is the relationship between her perceptions of her Chinese heritage and American realities. For the Chinese American girl, the maddening paradox is that the same culture that produced the No-Name Woman (the aunt who drowned herself in the family well) and Moon Orchid (the aunt who ends up insane)O also produced Fa Mu Lan (the woman warrior) and Brave Orchid (the mother who defies the subservient Chinese American female image). Fa Mu Lan uses the sword to avenge as in the classic, except her sword is her words. The Chinese American woman warrior must respond to the throat pain that returns unless she speaks the truth, to report crimes and to "talk story".

Because the American-born Chinese woman must confront dualities and contradictions, she is blessed with a special gift—"I learned to make my mind large, as the universe is large so that there is room for paradoxes" (p. 29).

The Woman Warrior is about a Chinese American woman's attempt to find her voice and fight the contradictions between Chinese and American culture. The novel is a celebration of strength and rejection of sentimentality and self-pity (Kim, 1981). The names of the characters in the novel are symbolic of the tension and struggle among Chinese immigrant women. Chinese American immigrant women are the women warriors who faced great odds and challenges in supporting families as they coped with poverty, survival in a male dominated Confucian society, and a racist America.

Mother Daughter Bonds: Family Saga

Stories of mother-daughter bonds are more abundant in contemporary literature which coincides with the women's movement and an increasing emphasis on connections. These stories celebrate the connections among women and their relationships, in contrast with classic Chinese stories which tend to emphasize the mother-son relationship with themes of family obligation and loyalty.

Western Fairy Tales: Triumph of the Daughter

Classic Western fairy tales typically portray the mother as the villain, and the mother-daughter relationship as competitive where the daughter replaces or is triumphant over the mother figure. Snow White, for example, is about an adolescent girl beset by her jealous stepmother, the queen, who tries to destroy her because she is more beautiful. When the queen issues an order to kill her, the servants instead abandon her in the forest, thus sparing her life. When the queen again tries to destroy her, the dwarfs rescue her. She finally succumbs to a deathlike sleep after tempted with a poisoned apple from her stepmother. A handsome prince falls in love with her beauty and rescues her. During the journey, the poisoned apple is jarred loose and Snow White regains consciousness. The queen dies (from jealousy), and the couple live happily ever after.

Cinderella, another favorite Western fairy tale, is also about a beautiful, patient, and modest adolescent girl who is forced to perform menial tasks and rejected by her two spoiled, haughty and heartless stepsisters. After Cinderella's mother has died; her father marries a cruel stepmother who is jealous of her beauty as an emerging adolescent. Unbeknownst to her stepmother and stepsisters, Cinderella attends the three-day celebration as a princess, during which the prince becomes enthralled with her. In her haste to leave the ball before midnight to avoid being transformed back to her original self in rags, she loses her glass slipper. The prince sets out to find his true love and the rightful owner of this slipper.

Like many Western fairy tales, there is competition and heightened rivalry between mother and daughter over who is more beautiful. The three days symbolize three stages of maturation or developmental tasks that Cinderella must go through before she achieves the maturity and integration of self to meet her prince face to face. These fairy tales typically split the good and bad mother figure. In Snow White, the good pre-Oedipal mother—all giving and protective—dies early on while the bad Oedipal mother—depriving, selfish, competitive, rejecting—is the jealous stepmother trying to deny Snow White an independent existence. The father figure is mostly absent or an ambivalent figure. Snow White must make her journey on her own (Heuscher, 1974).

These fairy tales portray beautiful females as innocent and naïve in passive and receptive roles. They are victim to the external forces besetting them in a journey of sexual maturation, separation and individuation. They are now being rewritten with females having greater strength and character without having to rely on prince charming to rescue her.

The Joy Luck Club: Bonds and Bondage

The *Joy Luck Club* (2000), a contemporary novel by Amy Tan, is about the lives of four Chinese American immigrant women and their daughters. The portraits of the intergenerational relationships illustrate the influence of culture and immigration on the psychological adjustment of the characters. They are slaves to their past, a fact that both bonds them together and puts them in bondage Historical Chinese culture and themes in this contemporary novel celebrate women as nurturing mothers, and capture the struggles, developmental crises, and character transformations of these women in evolving a bicultural identity. Two of the mother-daughter relationships are chosen for analysis here because they represent the rescue fantasy and warrior image of women, so characteristic in the fairy tales and myths being discussed.

The character of An-Mei Hsu portrays the rescue fantasy, the bondage of fate, and how the theme of separation and abandonment is recurrent through several generations. Born of the element water (symbolic of women), she is raised by her grandmother because her mother brought shame to the family. According to family lore, her mother ran off to marry a rich man after her husband died. An-Mei later discovers that her mother was actually raped, as a ruse to dishonor her, and to force her to marry this man so that she could bear him a son. Her mother returns to the dying grandmother; she cuts a piece of her flesh to be boiled in a medicinal soup, symbolic of the highest sacrifice of a daughter to her mother in a consciously fruitless attempt to heal. The boiling water scars An-Mei as she rushes to join her mother against her grandmother's wishes. She almost dies of suffocation, and it is grandmother's threat of abandonment that brings her back. An-Mei's mother later commits suicide (i.e., once again abandoning her) as the only way she knows to guarantee An-Mei's safe status in her husband's household; Chinese superstitious beliefs would force her husband to honor An-Mei forever or run the risk of retribution from her mother's spirit. In doing so, she achieves for her daughter in death what she could not do for her in life.

A motto in Chinese society is that it is better to die with honor than to live with shame. During Confucian society, a women's sanctity and honor belonged to her husband; rape marked the defilement of a woman's honor. During a time when women were without choices, it was not uncommon for women to choose suicide as a means to regain their honor.

The myth in An-Mei's family is that "an ancestor once stole water from a sacred well, and now water steals her son away"; this is An-Mei's explanation when her daughter's inattention results in her son being drowned at sea on a family outing. (It also symbolizes the family curse because her mother's rape brought shame onto to the family who then reject her, in the tradition of blaming women as sexual seducers while forgiving men for their impulsiveness and carnal desires.) An-Mei brings out the family Bible in a consciously fruitless attempt to bring her son back; she cries in despair for being so foolish to think she could use faith to change fate.

An-Mei rescues her daughter from her marriage to a white dermatologist. Her daughter, Rose, spends 17 years in a dependent, and unhealthy marriage whereby her husband constantly rescues her emotionally. In despair over her failing marriage and impending divorce, she attempts suicide. As An-Mei helps her daughter heal from her psychological pain, she is able to resolve her own issues of separation and abandonment. Mother and daughter plant a seedling together, nourished by water, symbolic of their new start. Since she was born without wood, this successful resolution rectifies that which her own mother was unsuccessful in, except through suicide. Rose is able to move from dependency to a healthy interdependence with her mother and comes to terms with her Chinese identity.

The character of Lindo Jong is a somewhat different portrayal of Chinese American women, more similar to the classic Chinese story of *Hua Mu Lan*, the Woman Warrior. Worried that her grandchildren will forget her, Lindo's mother gives her a gold bracelet, symbolic of the purity and genuineness of Chinese culture and character. Born without metal but of good character, Lindo comes from a poor upbringing, and is married into a well-to-do family at age 16 when her family is forced to leave (i.e., abandoning her) because of the floods. The marriage is loveless, and is not consummated. Unable to produce an heir, Lindo is blamed by her mother-in-law for being too balanced with the metal, meaning the gold which she brought with her to the marriage.

Given that divorce was taboo during these times, Lindo cunningly devises a way to capitalize on her in-laws superstitious beliefs and fears of social taboo. She fabricates a vision using information that she has astutely observed to predict that her marriage will be doomed unless it is immediately dissolved. Her in-laws believe her vision; they are all too willing to help her to leave the household to avoid the bad omen and fate predicted by her vision to befall her husband. Thus, she is freed from her marriage without shame or ostracism; her in-laws gratefully send her away to Beijing if she promises not to tell her story, an unusual accomplishment during those times in China. It is her cleverness, resoluteness and being true to herself that carry her through.

Lindo's daughter, Waverly, is crafty and snobbish like her mother. She is taught the *art of invisible strength* from her mother, that is, that the inner will is a dominant force. The mother-daughter relationship is one of battle, but fought through a battle of the wills. As Lindo says, the strongest wind cannot be seen (referring to the winds in mah-jong and martial arts). Waverly continues a silent battle with her mother over independence. Waverly develops her skills as a champion chess player in which she learns secret strategies from a neighbor. As she competes in tournaments and becomes the neighborhood heroine, she believes she is special (which is in contrast to the emphasis on modesty in Chinese culture). However, she is resentful of her mother's pride as an attempt to take credit for her accomplishments. When her mother modestly describes her winning as "luck", she views this as criticism.

She rebels after a confrontation only to lose her mother's silent support. Without her mother's support, she gives up the chess game and loses interest in winning. She finally comes to terms with her battle for independence from her mother, realizing it has been a battle fought within herself. What she saw "as a formidable foe in her mother, was now simply an old woman waiting for her daughter to come home" (Tan, 1989).

Lindo and her daughter Waverly are born with the elements of wind—symbolizing strategy and invisible strength; their relationship emphasizes power and competition. Lindo's developmental transformation is her ability to give up the fight with her mother.

This contemporary novel of women in Chinese immigrant families differs from their depiction in classical Chinese stories in that it portrays mothers as human beings with faults. Its portrayal of mother-daughter bonds also differs from the tendency to portray cross-gender parent-child relationships (father-daughter, mother-son, and husband-wife) in classical Chinese stories.

In the *Joy Luck Club*, Chinese culture continues to pervade the characters' lives while creating conflict with the influence of American culture in their lives. The Chinese American mothers continue to use Confucian moral principles and threats in their childrearing techniques. Lindo uses open criticism of Waverly's accomplishment—a common demonstration of Chinese modesty—to elicit compliments. Waverly misunderstands her mother's maternal pride and modesty as simple criticism, illustrating a common intergenerational misunderstanding in immigrant families.

Unlike the *Twenty-Four Stories,* the emphasis on maternal guidance is cause for tension between mothers and daughters in *The Joy Luck Club*.. As the daughters in this novel struggle for autonomy and identity, they rebel against maternal guidance and control. The mothers cannot understand the daughters' failure to abide by the mandate to be the obedient daughter.

Each generation grapples with the same dynamic issues faced by their mothers before—symbolized by the elements with which they were born and that determine their fate. Despite their initial disdain and rebelliousness against maternal expectations, the daughters come to realize how perceptive their mothers are and come to value what they have gained. The process is transforming in establishing their bicultural identity and mother-daughter bond.

The themes of loss and abandonment in An-Mei's story and the warrior images in Lindo's story are powerful cultural symbols and developmental themes as each negotiates the task of maturation. The appeal of this contemporary novel is in its symbolism of the five elements (Taoist concepts of fire, water, wood, earth, and metal), the celebration of mother-daughter bonds, and the creation of immigration legend. It demonstrates how biculturalism is an endpoint of transformation and independence.

Western Myths of Asian Women

The contemporary portrayals of Chinese American women in *The Joy Luck Club* and *The Woman Warrior* are popular among Chinese Americans because they emphasize women's strengths and end with admiration and pride, unlike many portrayals popular among Westerners about Asian women, including *Madame Butterfly, Sayonara, and Miss Saigon,* which portray Asian women as meek, subservient, and exotic. The latter stories end with pity for the heroine; they are tragedies whereby the Asian woman typically commits suicide following her unfulfilled union with the white male—that is, Asian women are abandoned and shamed. These stories mimic Asian values modesty, piety and honor, but are written from Western perspectives. Westerners often fail to understand how these portrayals victimize Asian women and deify white men.

Other 20th century stories about Asian women often featured them as prostitutes and losers. They were initially popular among Asian audiences because there were so few movies featuring Asian women as stars; they were later seen as offensive because they reinforced negative stereotypic myths and images of Asian women.

Madame Butterfly and Suzie Wong

Madam Butterfly (Puccini, 1904), *The World of Suzie Wong* (Quine, 1960), *Sayonara* (Logan, 1957), *and Miss. Saigon* (Schonberg, Maltby, & Boublil, 1990) are examples of contemporary movies and plays about Asian women in the periods following World War II and the Vietnam War. While Western audiences extol the exotic beauty and innocence of the Asian woman, and forgive her for selling her body, they nonetheless pity her. She is pathetic because the white world is not hers to share; she is innocent and foolishly committed to the white male soldier. She is ultimately the transient toy and sexual object for the American soldier before he returns to the *real woman* who is the object of his affection; in other words, she is abandoned for the white woman back home. After the war, the white male moves on while the Asian female mourns his loss; in her anguish or shame over losing the white man's love, she commits suicide. This is the myth about Asian women that Western filmmakers love to portray; it is the image that Western audiences retain.

The characters of Butterfly and her Captain Pinkerton illustrate this myth in the opera of *Madame Butterfly* by Puccilni (1904). Pinkerton, a dashing officer in the United States Navy, is also a philandering heel; he is infatuated with the 15 year old Butterfly, cognizant of her fragility, but is not "content with life unless he make his treasure the flowers on every shore." He says as he compares her to a butterfly, "I must pursue her even though I damage her wings." The stage for the tragedy is set. The beautiful Cio-Cio San has been a geisha, but is nonetheless fragile, unworldly, and in love with the handsome sailor. She deceives herself, despite abundant warnings, as to Pinkerton's motives.

"To die with Honor, when one can no longer live with Honor". It was in obscure ideographs; but it was also written on her father's kaimyo at the shrine, and she knew it well. She drew the blade affectionately across her palm. Then she made herself pretty with vermilion and powder and perfumes; and she prayed, humbly endeavoring at the last to make her peace. She had not forgotten the missionary's religion; but on

the dark road from death to Meido it seemed best now to trust herself
to the compassionate augustnesses, who had always been true.
Cho-Cho San from Madame Butterfly, Puccini's Opera.

This theme and myth about Asian women is repeated half a century later
in the play *Miss Saigon* (Schonberg et al., 1990), which revolves around Kim,
a young Vietnamese woman who is forced to work in a sex shop in Saigon.
She quickly falls in love with Chris, a marine guard at the U.S. embassy.
When Saigon falls to the Viet Cong, Chris--not realizing that Kim is
pregnant--is forced to retreat and abandon her. He returns home and
eventually marries a white woman. A few years later, he and his wife return
to find Kim who is now determined to make Chris take their son back to
the United States. Realizing her shame, she commits suicide to die with
honor.

Suzie Wong—the very name offends a generation of Asian Americans
who grew up in its shadow. While many today have not actually seen *The
World of Suzie Wong*, the 1960 movie directed by Richard Quine, what
matters is that after the film's release the most superficial (and offensive)
aspects of the Suzie Wong character singlehandedly usurped the image of
Asian womanhood in the Western imagination. Robert Lomax is a
struggling American artist who has moved to Hong Kong to learn whether
he can really paint. He meets Mee Ling, a tycoon's beautiful daughter,
onboard Hong Kong's Star Ferry. After checking into a local Wan Chai
hotel, he learns that the hotel is actually a brothel, and that Mee Ling is
actually Suzie Wong, the most popular prostitute in the place. Refusing to
accept Suzie because of her way of life, Robert's relationship with Suzie
begins as a purely artistic one, then becomes platonic friendship, then anger
tinged with hidden jealousy and internal conflict, then passionate love, and
finally an acceptance of her as a complete person, but not without tragic
consequences.

In the Asian American consciousness, the two most offensive images
are Suzie Wong and Madame Butterfly because they degrade Asian women
as prostitutes and insult Asian men by implying that only Caucasian men are
worthy objects of love (Nahm, 2003). They marginalize and place into
bondage the women they define; Chinese American women were called
"Suzie" for years after the movie's release.

Bicultural Identity: Be Chinese! You are an American!

Chinese immigrant families emphasize the importance of being Chinese in
their childrearing, while our American culture emphasizes the importance
of being American—This is the contradiction.

Flower Drum Song

The *Flower Drum Song* was one of the first contemporary movies to portray Asian women and men in positive roles and positions of strength in a musical romantic comedy. Mei Li, a sweet, modest Hong Kong picture bride arrives to marry Sammy Fong, a nightclub owner who is in love with Nancy Low, a sultry, brassy showgirl. The contrast between the "traditional" versus "modern" woman captures the dichotomous images of Chinese American women and the essence of achieving a cultural identity. Mei Li falls in love with Ta, who is more interested in Nancy Low, much to his father's disapproval. As the couples struggle with their choice of a mate in marriage, the challenges of biculturalism are played out.

As Ta's father insists, his mandate for Ta to be Chinese and pick the perfect Chinese wife is strong—embodied in Mei Li. Yet as Sammy Fong and Nancy Low realize, they are who they are, influenced by Western ways. Unfortunately, the story reinforces the notion that the choice is to be either Chinese of American instead of showing the ability to evolve a bicultural identity.

Creating Immigration Legends

Contemporary stories offer images of strong women compared to classic Chinese stories which celebrate their beauty, ruthlessness, or deceit. As Chinese Americans, contemporary stories now written from an Asian perspective by Asian writers (e.g., Crouching Tiger, Hidden Dragon and The Joy Luck Club) offer positive images of Asian American women which counter degrading and offensive images prevalent in Western society of the exotic, subservient Chinese female or Chinese prostitute. These stories capture the complexity of Chinese values, celebrate the strengths of Chinese culture, and provide meaning for life's journey. As Chinese immigration evolved from the early Chinese immigrants of the 1850s from the farming villages of Toisan who were sojourners to the later Cantonese Chinese immigrants from Hong Kong reuniting with families in the U.S. to the now mixed immigration of Chinese from Taiwan, Fuchow, and many parts of China, the mandate to "never forget we are Chinese" remains strong. It is a source of bonding and connections, a protection against the onslaughts of discrimination in the U.S., and a pride of belonging to promote resilience. Out of these experiences, Chinese American families can each have their own family saga and create their immigration legend to sustain them as they travel their journey to the West.

There are many myths in the Chinese American story. Racism and anti-Chinese exclusion immigration policies, violence against Asians for stealing jobs led to beliefs among the early Toisanese Chinese immigrants that they could not make it in a white man's world. These beliefs were fueled by experiences denying them access, negative and disempowering media images of Asian men and women. There are beliefs about following the traditional as bad and the modern as good. These myths can marginalize and place into bondage the people they define; we need them to be the fabric that bonds and connects, heals and nurtures. We need these legends to provide the continuity through the generations, to celebrate strength and empower immigrant families to go forward to develop a bicultural identity. In drawing on mythology and stories, each family can create its own immigration legend to empower them and the generations that follow.

Having Face: Teaching Family Loyalty and Obligation

To look at creating immigration legend, we should look at what Chinese immigrant families teach. A core principle is having face or *yu meen*. This principle is reinforced in daily life through admonitions that someone *hmn pa chew*, i.e. not afraid of shame. Avoiding shame within the Asian culture is intricately tied to a sense of pride. It is linked to modesty as those who brag too much have no shame. Failure is magnified because it means bringing shame on the entire family (e.g., the saga of An Mei in Joy Luck Club whose mother was raped).

A second core principle is that of maintaining a Chinese identity. Children are often taught to be proud of the 5000 years of Chinese culture and achievements compared to the paltry 300 years of American culture. This often is at odds in a society that may demand loyalty oaths in the form extreme American patriotism in schools and society during the McCarthy anti-communist era. Or the subtle or not so subtle emphasis on true Americans being white, and all Chinese being foreigners. This principle is reinforced in the celebration of white American culture as being normative. American history is taught as beginning with the arrival of the Pilgrims on Plymouth Rock.

Loyalty to the group or family is a third core principle as brothers are expected to protect their sisters. Obligation to the welfare of the family is prominent as elder children often make sacrifices for the well being of their younger siblings. A parent's duty to the family is held as among the highest virtue.

Golden Mountain Myth: The Search

America the Beautiful, the land of opportunity! These were the words we heard as Toisanese immigrants. *Fah Kay*, i.e., Flowered Flag or *Mei Kuo*, i.e., Beautiful Country was the name for the U.S. given by the Toisanese Chinese immigrants. The image of the U.S. was *Gum* San or Golden Mountain. Chinese immigrants heard of the Golden Mountain set in the hills of San Francisco during the California Gold Rush where it was said that men could pick gold off the streets. The myth grew as the Chinese dreamed of immigrating to the Golden Mountain and return to China as rich men. As the early Chinese sojourners toiled to build the railroads and mined the gold dust left behind by the white gold miners, they perpetuated the myth to their families back home. Their search for a fortune left them poor with few opportunities to return to China, much less as rich men. They embellished their stories to themselves and to their wives, in order to ease the pain of poverty and racism faced here in America.

Melting Pot Myth: The American Dream

This vision of America in turn perpetuated the Melting Pot Myth, the belief that we would be one people, that we are an immigrant nation, and that it was a land of equal opportunity, that all men are created equal, and you can become an American. It was a myth because, in a race conscious society, you needed to be white and "to look American" to fully access the fruits of opportunity. Yet, the Melting Pot Myth was taught in schools and pounded into speeches. This denial that race matters created generations of Americans who doubted their identities and selves; it created the mistaken that belief that if you did not get something, it was because you did not work hard enough. We have come to realize that the American Dream was limited to those who are white, and that this needed to be rectified. In the words of Martin Luther King, in his famous 1963 speech on the steps of the Lincoln Memorial, is the legend yet to be realized: *"I have a dream deeply rooted in the American dream. I have a dream that this nation will rise up one day, and live out the true meaning of its creed. We hold these truths to be self-evident, that all men are created equal."*

The New Colossus: Statue of Liberty

Not like the brazen giant of Greek fame,
With conquering limbs astride from land to land,
Here at our sea-washed, sunset-gates shall stand
A mighty woman with a torch, whose flame
Is the imprisoned lightning, and her name
Mother of Exiles. From her beacon-hand
Glows world-wide welcome, her mild eyes command
The air-bridged harbor that twin-cities frame.

"Keep, ancient lands, your storied pomp!" cries she,
With silent lips. "Give me your tired, your poor,
Your huddled masses yearning to breathe free,
The wretched refuse of your teeming shore;

> Send these, the homeless, tempest-tost to me,
> I lift my lamp beside the golden door!"
> *Emma Lazarus. November, 2, 1883*

The "New Colossus", the famous sonnet written by Emma Lazarus in 1883, has been affixed to the inner walls of the pedestal the Statue of Liberty since the early 1900's. It has come to symbolize the statue's universal message of hope and freedom for immigrants coming to America and people seeking freedom around the world. The Statue of Liberty is more than a monument. Called the *Copper Lady* by Chinese immigrants, it is one of the most universal symbols of political freedom and democracy. It is the gateway to New York City, and the place to which we take tourists from out of town. It is the place from which the intergenerational saga begins.

CHAPTER 3: CULTURAL BONDS AND SYMBOLS

As Chinese culture stresses the use of metaphors and symbolism, food and words become highly symbolic in capturing its essence and its values. The partaking of food is to ingest the properties and characteristics that the dishes and their ingredients confer or symbolize—often associated with propitious wishes to be healthy, wealthy, and wise.

Animals of the Chinese zodiac, in particular, are valued for the attributes they have. They are often present as symbols in ceremonies and rituals as in the martial arts where movements are named after animals as metaphors for the power they produce. People are believed to acquire the attributes of the Chinese zodiac animal for the year in which they are born. Their presence in dishes are intended to confer the power they embody or propitious wishes they confer. These symbols become part of the food rituals which form the family and cultural bonds and connections among us.

Nurturing our Bodies and Souls

The Immortal Peach vs. The Forbidden Apple

In the Bible, God planted the Garden of Eden in the East. He told Adam, "You may eat of all the trees in the garden. You are not to eat from thihe tree of knowledge, of good and evil; on the day you eat of it, you shall most surely die". It is woman, Eve, who tempts man, Adam, to eat the apple, the forbidden fruit (Genesis 1:1:24).

In Taoism and Buddhism, a peach tree grows on Jade Mountain of the *Hsi Wu Mu* (Queen Mother of the West). It blooms once every 3000 years, so is a symbol of long life. Those who eat its fruit gain immortality. It is

Monkey who steals the peach of immortality, and was banished from heaven (Book of Mountains and Sea).

The apple in the Garden of Eden is a symbol of earthly desires and temptation; it is a fruit from the tree of knowledge, and also represented Christ and the divine wisdom. The peach from the Jade Mountain of the West is a symbol of great importance in China; it symbolizes longevity and immortality. T'ao, the Chinese word for "peach", is a homonym for marriage; consequently, the peach is considered propitious for marriage. Because it blooms early, it also symbolizes fertility (Gibson, 1996).

From the time of creation, food has come to symbolize the bonds among people, more than the sustenance needed to keep us alive and healthy. In the West, the emphasis is on earthly temptation and relationship between man and woman. In the East, the emphasis is on immortality, procreation and the mother-son relationship.

Food Rituals: Harmony and Bonding

While food is often considered a universal bond, food rituals vary widely across cultures, and have great significance in reflecting a culture's values and beliefs. Tea, for example, is common in the rituals of several cultures. The tea ceremony in Japanese culture is a sacred ceremony conducted in silence to honor an esteemed guest. *Dim Sum* (little pleasures) or *yum cha* (drinking tea) in Chinese culture is ritualized as a Sunday brunch and time to make conversation and connections with family, friends, and relatives at teahouses. High tea, taken during the afternoon in British culture is typically accompanied by serving simple cookies or cake with a few friends.

Sharing a meal is a common bonding experience for people in most cultures. While Westerners "break bread together", Chinese will "eat rice together"; thus, "Have you eaten rice yet?" in Chinese is comparable to the American "Hello". Food is at the heart of our cultural rituals to celebrate our children, our ancestors, and ourselves—through banquets in the Chinese culture. Birthday banquets generally have a dish of long noodles or *cheung mein*, a homonym for "long life" or longevity. Names of other dishes are homonyms for propitious characteristics—*tze gee tau* or lion's head made of pork balls; *chern ga fook* or entire family prosperity made of mixed vegetable, meats, and seafood; *bat bow fan* or eight precious treasures rice; *yin yang* rice; dragon and phoenix platter made of lobster and chicken; and *fot gow* or prosperity cake. Good fortune befalls those who partake—to become healthy, wealthy, and wise. Reverence is bestowed on those to whom it is offered—including our ancestors.

Balancing Ying and Yang: Health

In Chinese philosophy, the feminine principle of yin is the dark, moist, shadowy and receptive power (i.e., moon) that is also creative while the masculine principle of yang (i.e., sun) is the bright, hot, powerful creative energy. Balance of these principles is essential to life; it is the yin that brings all the yang stirrings into manifestation. Purging and fasting has been used to balance these energies within a person, and to drive out the evil spirits or bad winds. Western cultures associate mother earth and heavenly father as feminine and masculine opposing principles. Healing in Asian cultures involves the restoration of bodily health while healing in Western culture is the excision and suppression of disease—germs, toxins or fever. For Chinese, this means restoring the yin-yang balance the use of herbal soups and tonics.

Dragons, Phoenix, Tigers—Yin and Yang Power and Protection

In prizing the mystical and magical as in the martial arts, Chinese culture also prize mythical animals—most often the dragon, phoenix, and tiger. The Chinese Dragon is often seen as the symbol of divine protection and vigilance. It is regarded as the supreme being amongst all creatures. It has the ability to live in the seas, fly up the heavens and coiled up in the land in the form of mountains. Being a divine mythical animal, the dragon can ward off wandering evil spirits, protect the innocent and bestow safety to all that hold his emblem. The dragon is said to have nine resemblances; there

are five types of dragons with the celestial dragon representing joy, health, and fertility. It is protective, in contrast to the Western image of the dragon as negative and satanic and representative of destructive power and defiler of innocence.

The phoenix is considered to be the empress of birds and one of the four sacred creatures whose presence appears in times of peace and prosperity. It remains hidden at other times; its divine origin from the sun or fire connecting it with the south. The dragon and phoenix are frequently depicted together, personifying the unity of yin and yang or male and female. The dragon is a male solar symbol representing happiness, while the phoenix is a female lunar symbol of prosperity and the Chinese empress. Commonly used as a theme in wedding celebrations, the dragon and phoenix (served as lobster and chicken) are linked as animals that bring happiness, health, and fertility.

Tigers are not native to China, and so were treated as mythical beasts.

The tiger is regarded as the fiercest of beasts and also considered the king of all wild beasts—contrary to the West, where the lion is considered the king of beasts. The stripes on its head are imagined to form the character *wang*, meaning king (Scott, 1980, pp.33-36). Courageous, aggressive and adventurous to extremes, the tiger is considered sensitive and generous to loved ones. Admired for its playful personality, it is compatible with dragons, horses and dogs. In Chinese culture, the tiger represents vital animal energy, power, ferocity, royalty, and thus, protection. The tiger protects graves and is a Chinese guardian of hunting. The white tiger has *yin* (female) attributes and opposes the dragon. Because it can see in the dark, it symbolizes illumination and the new moon. Tigers also have *yang* (male) attributes and signify the way and valor.

Thus, the tiger and dragon are symbols of opposing but complementary strength and power as demonstrated in the movie, *Crouching Tiger, Hidden Dragon,* and of the hidden power and strength of Lindo Jong in *The Joy Luck Club (2000).*

Turtle and Monkey—Longevity and Intelligence

Among the earthly animals of the Chinese zodiac, the turtle (or tortoise) is believed to carry the world or to represent the cosmos with its upper shell being the heavens, its body the earth and its under shell the water or underworld. It is a symbol of longevity, indestructibility and immortality (Gibson, 1996, p.107). The monkey represents fantasy, intelligence, and cunning; he is a trickster figure embodying base human nature. His magical powers and mischievousness is legendary in *Journey to the West.*

The Lion Dance—Bringing Good Fortune

The Chinese use the lion dance as a vehicle for dispensing all the good blessings of heaven to the community and for guarding against misfortune. The dance is performed not only during Lunar New Year celebration but also on auspicious occasions (e.g., weddings), and represents the hopes and aspirations of the Chinese people for all the good things life holds. The Lion Dance (http://a2amas.com/liondance/) begins in a cave, behind a closed portal, with a sleeping lion. An overweight Buddhist monk enters, looks around and prepares the shrine. He lights a lantern, opens the portal's double doors, sweeps away the dust and leaves, and lights candles and incense burners. He wakens the lion with a drum and gong and they play.

Eventually the monk tries to entice the lion to pray before the altar, but the lion has other plans. When the lion gets bored, the monk teases him with some greens, which makes the lion angry, so he subsequently bites the monk. The lion then takes the greens from the monk and eats them. Sometimes additional greens are hung out of the lion's reach. The lion disperses the greens onto the audience three times, giving them the blessings of health, wealth and good fortune. After a nap, the lion is ready to play again, but the monk has left, leaving the lion to dance by himself before backing into the cave.

In Chinese culture, the lion is said to possess mystical properties. When paired with the five colors (yellow, black, green, red and white) of his costume, the lion is said to have control over the five cardinal directions. The costume is composed of many symbolic shapes. The bird shaped horn represents the phoenix. The ears and tail are of the unicorn. The protruding forehead, adorned with a mirror that deflects evil forces, and the long beard are characteristic of Asian dragons. The lion walks back and forth, in a zigzag path, in order to confuse evil spirits, which the Chinese believe move in straight lines. Finally, the act of eating and dispersing of the greens symbolizes the distribution of wealth and good fortune to all those present.

The Chinese Banquet—Healthy, Wealthy, and Wise

The Chinese banquet is traditional and full of ritual, intended to demonstrate abundance by the number and quality of dishes, generosity of the host, harmony and balance in the choice of dishes, and bonding in its execution and decorum.

The value placed on harmony and balance in the Chinese culture is played out in the Chinese banquet—perfected to an art form. In a perfect Chinese banquet, all the dishes are in harmony with one another, balancing ingredients, tastes, and order of presentation. Ingredients in a dish are balanced in color, texture, shape, and flavor. There are nine or ten dishes, symbolizing longevity or supreme; the lobster and chicken dishes are served in the middle (according to Cantonese cuisine) symbolizing the juxtaposition of the Dragon and Phoenix, and the balance of yin-yang properties.

As children, we followed these customs and practices, we enjoyed the banquet food, but did not understand the full meaning of the various foods. As adults, we came to believe they would make us healthy, wealthy, and wise.

Harmony and Completeness: Chicken and Fish

As a child, I was sent to buy a fish once. The *fishman,* as my mother would call him, removed the head while cleaning it. My mother was so upset that she sent me to return the fish; she considered it incomplete; it was not whole. I remember feeling mortified because I thought the *fishman* would laugh at me. To my great relief, the *fishman* understood and gave me another fish.

My mother would always admonish us to finish our rice especially during the Lunar New Year's since it would be a bad omen during the coming year if we didn't. Somehow it meant that something bad would happen to us. We never really knew what that would be but we always complied. Then she would always say that we would end up marrying a pock-faced husband if we didn't finish our rice.

This emphasis on wholeness and completeness symbolizes the importance of harmony in the Chinese culture and the sense of imbalance and impending doom when it is not there. Only as an adult could I begin to appreciate how these rituals and practices helped to provide the feelings of security, integrity, and plenty in one's life. The ambivalent feelings we experienced as children were part of the bicultural struggle. It combined the sense of uniqueness and connection amidst the struggle of being viewed as different, exotic, or alien.

The harmony and balance necessary in life and in Chinese culture is often represented by the wholeness of the chicken we served. It was always important in our family and other Chinese families to have a whole chicken at all celebrations and rituals. The bland and simple white chicken served during funeral dinners represents mourning, while the decorated or roasted chicken served during birthdays and weddings represents happiness and celebration. Although it was not customary or necessary for my parents to buy birthday presents for us as children, they were sure to serve a chicken to celebrate our birthdays. Unfortunately, we often preferred the present.

Fish was important, not only because it can be served whole, but also because the Chinese word for fish—*yau yee*—is a homonym for abundance. Later on, we discovered that fried squid, or *chow yau yee,* pronounced in a slightly higher tone, might be used as code to announce to the eater that he or she was going to be fired from his or her job. This play on words is common to Chinese eating habits, and in the naming of food dishes.

Prosperity and Fate (*Herng Fook*): Wealth

Owning land is a measure of prosperity in Chinese culture. My father bought a half-acre of land in Islip, New York, way out on Long Island. Since we rarely ventured outside New York City, this was "the country"; he was going to get us out of the ghetto He was going to build a country home; this land was the promise of a dream that would remain unfulfilled. while he never built on this land, it symbolized his attainment of prosperity here in America as we spent many weekends visiting it while he cleared trees for a future home.

Growing up, our living quarters were modest and small not unlike that of most Chinese immigrants. At family and social events, this meant that children were generally within earshot of the conversation of our elders. We were educated indirectly from listening to these conversations about *tiel meng* or one's life and fate, and how some people were *ji-woon* (unlucky) while others were *herng-fook* (prosperous). Not much could be done about fate. The elders endlessly bemoaned their fate in America, struggling to make a living. Amidst this anguish were their dreams of returning to China for retirement to live in comfort and with respect in their home villages. This was the perpetual dream of my father as he hoped to make the hardship and struggle of working in a laundry more bearable. The elders would commiserate together, believing there was no escape from their fate of struggle and poverty, a kind of bondage. The dream of returning to an idyllic China with the most tasty and fresh fruit and the most beautiful flowers and scenery that far surpassed any in America was the illusion of the peach orchard in the Jade Mountain of their minds.

It was the dream of my father and that of the Chinese elders not to toil so hard in laundries 12 hours a day 6 days a week, and to return to China in their retirement while they criticized the injustices of American society. As children, we would pooh pooh my father, always challenging him, never believing him. Tired of hearing these empty dreams, we would tell him, "Why don't you go back; you'll hate it there.", never realizing his bondage and his inability to escape his fate here in America. In 1972, at the age of 72, he made his trip back to China 40 years after he left; he found he no longer belonged. He returned with failing health, his dreams dashed, and died two years later.

In an immigrant community where most were poor, small differences were often important markers of social status. Many Toisanese immigrants had come with few of their possessions; most had little of value to bring. As peasants born in poverty, 24K gold was valued not only for their monetary value, but also for its ability to be converted to cash. Unlike paper money, gold was not subject to depreciating value as a result of political and government turmoil. Twenty-four carat gold in the form of jewelry was a means of demonstrating one's prosperity as well as providing nuggets of security since it could be melted down in times of need.

The jade heart is often one of the first gifts of jewelry that Chinese mothers give to their daughters. In Chinese culture, jade is often worn as an amulet to protect one from harm and evil; it is believed to have protective powers. My mother always told the story of a woman who fell from a two- story window; the jade she was wearing broke but she was unharmed. My mother ensured that gold and jade would be part of our dowry as did most Chinese immigrant mothers.

The power of these maternal gifts is immensely symbolic. When I was a young teen, a man exposed himself to me while I was traveling on a New York City subway. Frightened by the experience, my mother gave me a wad of black pepper wrapped in wax paper secured with a rubber band (this was before the days of pepper spray). I was told to throw this in someone's face if I was ever threatened again. For years, I walked around with this gift from my mother in my pocketbook with the illusion of feeling safe and protected. It was not until many years later that I wondered what I would have said if assaulted: "Wait, I have to get this pepper out of my bag so that I could mace you." By the time I opened my bag, found the pepper, removed the rubber band, and threw it in the person's face as I had been instructed to do, it would probably have been too late. But it was my mother's words and the symbol of her protection that made me feel safe.

Diligence (*Qin*) and Industry: Wisdom

Given the hardships of the laundry (and now the restaurants), Chinese parents placed their hopes and dreams on their children. While the opportunity for them to escape the laundry was viewed as futile, they placed their faith on a better future for their children.

And so we were always told to study industriously, or *keen let duk shee* so that we would not have to suffer working in a laundry. To be as wise as the scholars in China, and this would bring the respect and economic rewards. Books and the pursuit of academic achievement were valued. Because scholarly study was typically reserved for men, it was difficult for my parents to understand as I went on for my doctorate. My father expected me to go to work after I finished high school, and to contribute financially to the family until I married. This was their pension since there was no social security in China.

At each step of my academic progress toward a higher degree, my parents expressed a mix of surprise, dismay, and pride. My father pondered the futility of an education for females if they were only get married and have children; but then, this was America! At the same time, becoming a scholar wase considered the height of achievement. But then, what was psychology anyway. When I first tried to explain to my mother in Chinese why my education was taking so many years, and what psychology was, she finally smiled. "Oh, you are going to be a brain surgeon,:" she said, since I had explained that psychology was the study of the mind to examine and heal.

My parents' contradictory outlook and quandary reflected the challenges faced by Chinese immigrant families in a racist society. Many resorted to academic and scholarly pursuits, which fit with Confucian values, as a means of social and economic advancement. Our concise verbal styles, which were valued in Chinese culture, together with learning English as a second language channeled many toward the sciences and engineering.

Celebrations

Celebrations are the occasions for special foods and dishes with symbolic meaning prepared for different Chinese festivals and life events—always to promote health, prosperity, and wisdom; harmony and balance are central to the meal including how certain foods confer not only the nutritional properties, but also the symbolic properties. I remember a special occasion when my parents and their friends had captured or bought a mountain lion to be cooked for dinner. Because the Chinese always want their food to be at its freshest, the live mountain lion was caged in the living room waiting to be slaughtered. All the children cautiously approached to see it. I remember our awe of this wild beast, but limited understanding of why there was this big fuss over this poor animal. We did not realize how rare mountain lion is as a food item; nor did we appreciate the value of it power, energy, and courage attributes that would be conferred to the eater. The following excerpt captures the experience.

Drinking Tiger Soup

When I was six or seven, my mother's aunt gave me a broth made of tiger bone. She promised it would cure my asthma and turn me into a robust child. My mother, a great believer in ancient remedies, readily consented.

"You are lucky," Great Aunt told me, as she poured the steaming black broth into a bowl. "With all the bombings, there aren't that many tigers left in our country. You, boy, might be drinking the bones of the last one." Our country was Vietnam.

I watched the soup billowing smoke in front of me, and felt as if I was about to swallow poison. To make things worse, the tiger was my favorite animal and I was certain I was wholly unworthy to receive such a sacrifice. But a Vietnamese child is obedient; I wept, but I drank.

Andrew Lam (1996)

Red Eggs: Creation

Upon the birth of a child, Chinese parents will celebrate the one-month birthday of the child, especially if it is a boy. Given the high rate of infant mortality in China, newborns and postnatal mothers stayed at home for the entire month. Special tonics are prepared including a special chicken soup spiced with gin and ginger, and pig trotters vinaigrette with eggs and peanuts to help the postpartum mother restore her strength. A one-month banquet may include the dish of red colored eggs to symbolize the celebration of creation. The newborn receives monetary gifts in red envelopes or 24 carat gold jewelry from the relatives as wished of happiness and prosperity.

The Chinese Wedding: Rituals and Contrasts

The Chinese wedding is celebrated with the color red and many symbols of fertility, longevity, and harmony—to bear children, live a long life, and promote harmony between husband and wife. Growing up Chinese American, our means were modest, and we struggled to make ends meet. Yet true to Chinese tradition, my mother was intent on buying jewelry for our dowry to make sure we "have face" when we married. She emphasized fairness for my sister and me, always cautioning us never to fight among ourselves over material things. Two of her most treasured and classic pieces of jewelry were the 24-carat gold *lung fung* (dragon-phoenix) bangle bracelets, and the jade heart. Almost every Chinese American bride gets one, and we were to be no different.

A camphor-type hope chest is also commonly part of the dowry among Chinese Americans. Since Chinese goods were less common in the U.S. and hard to find without paying a lot, it was common practice for immigrants arriving from China to make purchases for those who were already here. Consequently, my mother went through pains to ask relatives and friends arriving from China to purchase them items so that we would have a proper dowry. When my hope chest arrived, it turned out to be a mahogany chest with mother of pearl inlaid depicting a dragon and phoenix. If I had to have a hope chest, I wanted a carved wood chest with a simple design. I initially hated its gaudiness since I was into the simplicity of Scandinavian design at the time. I hated this chest so much that I would cover it up believing my mother just did not understand or have the proper taste. Twenty years later, I found this chest to be quite beautiful providing contrast and aesthetic interest against the plainness of my Scandinavian furniture.

These rituals, symbols and our struggles with them are uniquely Chinese American. Chinese weddings were the place where the differences stand in stark contrast and contradiction between Western and Chinese cultures. The white wedding gown, a symbol of purity and virginity in Western culture stands in antithesis to the red satin embroidered wedding gown, a symbol of celebration and fertility in Chinese culture. In the West, red is flamboyant while in the East, white is for mourning.

There are several defining moments when we first began to celebrate weddings within the family. My sister, *Fay Hah*, was the first to marry. We stood in awe when her future in-laws sent over a whole succulent roast pig complete with the apple in the mouth after the engagement as a symbol of their acceptance and pleasure with the future daughter-in-law. As a symbol of prosperity and generosity of the groom's family, this was accepted with great pleasure by my parents. Another roast pig and a monetary dowry followed 3 days after the wedding since this is traditionally the first time the bride is allowed to return home to visit her parents. At my brother *Sel Teng*'s wedding, coconut heads were delivered to our family by the bride's family along with other gifts as a way to honor my father as the new father-in-law and head of the family; coconut or *year how* in Chinese is a homonym for father-in-law's head. We chuckled at the double entendre of these symbols. My future mother in-law was in Hong Kong at the time of my wedding and could not be present at the ceremony; my husband and I were represented at the wedding banquet she held in Hong Kong by two chickens.

Other wedding customs include the presentation of a wild goose as the symbol of marital harmony and fidelity; these birds mate for life and migrate together. Because wild geese are difficult to obtain, chickens have been used as an alternative. Fruits and nuts are frequently offered as gifts to symbolize fertility and wishes for the couple to bear many children. Peanuts *(sheng)* a homonym for birth, and dates *(zaozi)* a homonym for "early arrival of a male son" are often placed inside the new quilt on the marital bed.

Lunar New Year: Family Bonds

The Lunar New Year Festival is a time of great celebration in Chinese culture, more important than Christmas or Thanksgiving in American culture. Celebrations continue for several weeks with visits to friends and relatives bearing pastries and sweets made especially for Chinese New Year. If symbolism is important in eating among Chinese, it is even more so during Lunar New Year. Great preparation is needed to bring in the New Year. One must have a clean house and clean body; one must resolve all debts; one cannot do chores on New Year's Day.

My mother would spend weeks preparing these pastries, as would all the other Chinese American mothers and grandmothers. We would spend hours together kneading the dough and forming the wrappers to be filled with sugar and peanuts or *fah sheng* symbolizing "sweet life". A popular New Year dessert is *nien gao*, a sweet steamed glutinous rice pudding, a homonym for the "year will soar high". My mother often made extra pastries, especially for the men whose wives were not in the U.S. to make it for them. I have memories of how she would beam with pride when she was complimented about how good they tasted; yet, she would modestly claim that they were only so-so.

Lunar New Year is a time of constant feasting with dishes symbolizing longevity, prosperity, and happiness. New Year's Eve is a night of feasting while New Year's Day is a day of fasting, that is, eating *lo horn ji,* a vegetarian dish out of respect for all living animals. It is expected that one must have only good thoughts, have no arguments, finish all of one's rice, and be especially careful not to break anything in order to usher in the New Year. We would comply to ensure that the year would be propitious and that no harm would befall us. My parents, as did all our relatives, always gave us *hung bao* (red envelopes) filled with money New Year's Day with money in it to wish us prosperity and good fortune.

Following New Year's Day, all families must officially *hoy neen,* or open the year by having a dinner banquet for the extended family. On this occasion, my father always emphasized how we only used *jing-sick-toy-lieu* (the most genuine of ingredients) in creating the dishes. He would proudly claim how we did not scrimp on ingredients in our home cooking the way they did in restaurants; we used only the best ingredients. Rituals were followed in preparing this 10-course banquet. Special dishes were served, each one a homonym for some auspicious wish for prosperity, happiness, or longevity, each one symbolizing some desirable attribute. Before sitting down to dinner, the food is presented as a sacrifice before the picture of our ancestors. There was the dish with black fungus or *fot toy* symbolizing prosperity; the bean curd dish or *foo juk* to take away the bitterness; the *see goo* or radish dish to make our events turn out well; the bean vermicelli or *fun see* dish so that we might all find our fortune; and the jujubes or *hung do* dish to celebrate the happiness. Of course, we could not do without the whole chicken and fish symbolizing unity and completeness, or a "favorable start and finish".

As children, we loved and looked forward to Lunar New Year. Every year, my mother would explain once again the meaning of each of the different foods used to prepare the New Year dinner. Each year, we would listen as if it were the first time. There were no unpleasant words or thoughts to be spoken. If any of us said something inauspicious by accident, she would say, *chick gaw lai see*, a Chinese version of *gezunheit* to neutralize the bad thought. All of this meant so much to my mother, and ultimately to all of us as she emphasized the completeness and circularity of life. She frequently reminded us of how every person comes full circle, and follows in the footsteps of one another.

My mother never fully knew the customs in detail not having had her mother for much of her childhood; however, she kind of made them up along the way. When we started to question a practice or symbol in too much detail, she would resort to saying, "Let's just say it is good." She would often explain that it was to have *yuan*, a term for "roundness" suggesting the attainment of what are commonly known as the Five Happinesses: long life, wealth, peace, virtue, and honor. Having *yuan* also suggests family unity and harmony, and the unity of society—this was her goal.

Christmas and Thanksgiving, on the other hand, was just another day since these holidays bore little significance in the Chinese culture. As we got older, we insisted that we celebrate it "just like everybody else". Then, my mother decided we would celebrate by serving a fresh-killed whole chicken--her symbol of a celebration. As we got older, my sister and I decided we would celebrate Christmas ourselves, and began our custom of exchanging presents. We decorated a small, artificial Christmas tree; we too made up our own rules. We always opened our presents soon after we got them instead of waiting for Christmas. Then we would carefully rewrap them and keep them under the tree until Christmas. My mother tolerated these Western holidays for our sake; at her suggestion, we began to keep the presents wrapped under the Christmas tree until February to celebrate Lunar New Year. We never thought this was odd; we were just being Chinese American.

Celebrating Our Ancestors: Reinforcing Our Identity

Food rituals continue till death—the end of the journey. In Chinese culture, there is often not a hard line drawn between the sacred and secular, or between our earthly world and that of the gods—as in the adventures of

Monkey King and among the Greeks. In honoring spirits, gods, and ancestors, Chinese offer the same things that are useful in real life—food, entertainment, and money (Stepanchuk & Wong, 1991). Chinese American immigrants often altered these ceremonies to suit this new bicultural environment.

My mother was neither Buddhist nor Taoist; she supported the tenets of Christianity because she saw them aligned with Confucian moral teachings. After my father dies, she created a shrine in his honor. Following custom, she hung a large picture of my father over a table with Buddhist offerings; she periodically *baishen,* or "worshiped the spirits" to honor her ancestors Ah Gung, my grandfather, Dai Q, my maternal uncle, and my father. Her practices were not authentic and often modified for convenience; however they gave her peace and fulfilled her sense of obligation and loyalty to the family and my father. She was virtuous in being the good daughter and good wife. It puzzled us at first until we realized that it was the only way she knew to memorialize what she had and the journey she had taken. Not uncommon among Chinese American immigrants, she practiced these customs with more vigor and enthusiasm than even those in China.

In Chinese culture, a ten course meal follows the ending of a funeral for all mourners. The family will host this meal of *"white rice"* (as the color of mourning) to pay final respects to the deceased. Instead of the brightly colored dishes typical at banquets, a funeral meal will feature among its dishes a whole "white" chicken (poached chicken), "white" sweet cake, and the burning of incense.

The Chinese honor their ancestors in an annual journey to the cemetery during the *Qing Ming* festival in April, or "Clear and Bright day of remembrance". It corresponds with the onset of Spring; it is a time for family outings to tidy up the graves, remove weeds and sweep away leaves. While Westerners bring flowers, the Chinese bring feasts to the ancestral graves consisting of a chicken, roast meats, white rice wine, white sweet cake, and incense as their offerings; they then have a picnic at the gravesite.

Women as Healers

Chinese American immigrants continued their legacy through food to celebrate, to mourn and cope with loss, to adjust to immigration. Chinese immigrant women replicated the food and practices from China to provide the nurturance and connectedness. They celebrated with the special pastries and banquets, sustained the culture with the comfort foods from the village. In feeding the family, they united the family, mentored the next generation, forged bonds among clan and community members—they nurtured our bodies and our souls. Through food, they left their legacy as mothers and healers.

Food as health

Chinese soups, made from herbs and chicken, are considered tonics, which confer yin-yan properties and health benefits such as restoring balance to body fluids. So, my mother created the soups to heal our bodies and nurture our souls through illness and suffering; and so, she gave her gift of water to nurture and heal us, for us to fertilize and grow. Whenever we got cold sores or a cold, my mother would quickly boil some *lerng soup* (yin or cool tonic) for us to eliminate the *yeet hay* (heat). If she thought us to be *yerk* (weak) or unhealthy, she might *oon* (long slow braising) some gingseng, deer antlers, or other terrible tasting tonic. If we had a fever, out came the *kam woo* tea to bring it down. She would apply a camphor salve and have us sweat it out; my mother, like most Chinese families believed that the Western tradition of bringing down a fever with a tepid bath would kill us.

Health Tonics

Herbal soups (*yerk toy tong*) and tonics have played a distinct role in the healing practices within Chinese families throughout the generations. Basic essences of the body include: Qi (air), blood, and yin and yang qualities, which must be kept in balance in order to remain healthy. These are followed by pathologic factors of wind, moisture, and toxins, which cause illness. Deficiencies of yin will give rise to symptoms of dryness (e.g., dry mouth, cough) and heat (e.g., fever, inflammation) while deficiencies of yang give rise to symptoms of poor vitality and strength (e.g., fatigue, impotence), and lack of adequate warmth (e.g., chills). Deficiencies are caused by the failure of one to regulate the other (yin-yang).

Herbal soups are routinely served as part of a family meal. The yin, associated with water and female qualities, are used to balance an overabundance of yang, associated with fire and male qualities. Thus, the essence of female was transmitted through these herbal soups, providing nurturance to strengthen and restore vitality and health. While herbalists, who were commonly men, were known for their significant role as healers in traditional and Chinese American communities, it has been the women or wives and mothers who regularly prepared these soups. Loo and Yu (1984), in a 1979 survey of health practices among Chinese Americans in San Francisco, found that 95% of the respondents drank soups made with Chinese herbs; 23% drank it at least once a week, and 27% drank it at least once a month. Yin-yang qualities underlie the nutritional value of many foods and often dictate diet behaviors among Chinese families.

Animal parts are used for their healing properties in Chinese medicines and herbal tonics to restore health or to balance yin-yang qualities through their healing properties. Their value is enhanced depending on the specific conditions under which they are caught. For example, the value of deer antlers, used for herbal tonics, is increased if the deer is shot while running uphill or downhill according to my mother. It is believed that all the blood and nutrients rush to its head and antlers when the deer runs downhill. We always asked my mother how the seller could prove this. She would tell us only that we needed to trust and believe.

Since many Chinese immigrants immigrated from environments where infant mortality was high and starvation a reality, these tonics and soups provided their families with a means for dispelling evil spirits, toxins, and bad winds which caused us ill health. Though we were skeptical as we drank the tonics and ate the food, we felt that much stronger as we incorporated the characteristics my mother imparting in wishing us health, wealth, and wisdom.

Mooncakes: Celebration of Women

We can draw a parallel between the moon images in Chinese mythology of their fertilizing power and hidden strength and the images of Chinese American women immigrants as healers and nurturers through their food and herbal tonics. *Mooncakes* are eaten during August Moon Festival and offered up to the moonlight in honor of the moon mother; these are sweet pastries with egg yolks or sweet beans and nuts, representing fertility. We celebrate the moon as a reflection of female essence and symbolic of the great mother. Farmers and seafaring people, as were the Toisanese who were the first Chinese to immigrate to America in the 1850s, believe the weather changes with each new moon or when the moon passes the full phase. Moon goddesses were regarded as guardians of the waters, rivers, brooks, and springs which, gushing forth out of the ground, were usually held sacred to the goddess of fertility; probably because they so aptly symbolize that invisible hidden power of "bringing forth from within" which is the peculiar characteristic of feminine creation (Harding, 1971, p.111).

Words As Symbols: A Study Of Contrasts

Words of a language often capture the essence of a culture and its values. Whether it is the names of dishes in a Chinese banquet or Chinese poems used to convey good wishes, the use of metaphor and symbolism in the Chinese culture is high. There is an emphasis on brevity and the balance of words used in a Chinese couplet expresses the scholarly thought and moral teaching.

Obligation and Benevolence: The Sayings of Confucius and Mencius

Though she was not a Chinese scholar, my mother repeated the sayings of Mencius and Confucius to me. Like most Chinese American children, I heard the warnings, her advice, her wisdom and her moral teachings. like the foods she prepared, her words symbolized the dreams to which so many Chinese Americans aspire and the longing for what they left behind. I heard her voice.

Confucius and Mencius were Chinese philosophers in the 5th and 4th centuries B.C; both significantly influenced social and family relationships within Chinese culture. Confucius' sayings were both the object of awe and ridicule by Westerners. Picking up on the most superficial features of Confucianism, the Charlie Chan version of Confucian wisdom and fortune cookie sayings stereotyped American images of this Chinese philosopher. Yet Confucian teachings were the basis for moral teachings in most Chinese households.

Confucius' teachings were practical and ethical, rather than religious; they emphasized morality and proper social conduct based on the five virtues of kindness, uprightness, decorum, wisdom, and faithfulness, which constitute the whole of human duty, as described earlier in the *Twenty-Four Stories of Filial Piety*—one of his key concepts. Government and family relationships were paternalistic, with an emphasis on *li*, or ritual.

According to Confucius, there are five basic relationships in society that determines moral action and obligation: emperor-subject, father-son, husband-wife, elder brother-younger brother, elder friend-younger friend. All relationships are between a superior and subordinate; all demand obedience and learning proper behavior for one's role and status—resulting in the proper distribution of power and authority (see http://beatl.barnard.columbia.edu/reacting/china/confucianism.html#philosophy).

Mencius (372-289 B.C.) argued that all men have a mind that cannot bear to see the suffering of others. As a disciple of Confucius, he added compassion to moral education. His teachings assert that feelings of commiseration, shame, modesty, and approval/disapproval are essential to human beings because of their compassion. Mencius asserted that these feelings are correlated with principles of behavior and social conduct:

commiseration is the principle of benevolence; shame is the principle of righteousness; modesty is the principle of propriety; approval/disapprove is the principle of knowledge.

Style: Brevity is the Soul of Wisdom

Spring couplets are verses used by Chinese to suggest good fortune, longevity, or the birth of male offspring. Rules for composing a couplet are simple, but the art of composing these antithetical verses is a challenge. A couplet is made up of two lines of verse which are called the "head" and "tail" respectively, and should correspond with each other phonologically and syntactically word for word and phrase for phrase. For example,

> By virtue united, heaven is strong (de he gan geng)
> Through compassion shared, earth is yielding (ci tong kun shun)

The parallels between "virtue" and "compassion", "heaven" and "earth", "united" and "shared", "strong" and "yielding" serve the same purpose, and may be opposite in meaning. The brevity and concentrated meaning of the couplet is uniquely Chinese. It leaves out more than it says; through the visual quality of characters, it reveals a hidden dimension, which readers have to puzzle out themselves (Stepanchuk & Wong, 1991, p.12-13).

This emphasis on brevity, metaphor, and balance is the hallmark of Chinese scholarship. As children, we were always taught not to be too chatty, because virtuous women don't chat too much. We were cautioned to be quiet because "it did not look right", or that people would think "we had no shame". This contrasts with the Western standard in education, which expects us to raise our hand, speak up, and fight to be heard. We were taught that learning was a process of taking in information and listening; only fools did the opposite.

Scholarship in Western culture, by contrast, is often based on length and verbosity. While Westerners say, "A picture is worth a thousand words.", the Chinese might say, "A word could say a thousand things." Consequently, a couplet of eight words in Chinese could say more than 8 paragraphs in English.

The Power of Words: Chinese Names

What is in a name? We all have family names. For Westerners, it is a "last" name, while for Asians, it is placed first. Names have great symbolic significance in Chinese; they are chosen for their meaning to signify a character trait or a hope. Names typically have two radicals, with siblings sharing the same first radical to reflect their relationship; the second radical is distinctive; males may share a phrase when their names are linked together across several generations to reflect the ancestral bond.

Chinese have a tradition of giving names to mark important transition points in one's life. At times, it symbolized an attempt to change one's fate, to bring prosperity in times of adversity, to bring hope where there was none. Names mark the essence of our identities. As Chinese Americans, we have our Chinese names and our American ones. As children, we always understood and felt the differences in the names we were called. We took on the different characteristics, behaviors, and values associated with our different names.

And so, my mother was called *Tel* as a child; she changed her name to *May Yee* since she had lost her mother under the former name. She used *Jung Fung Gor*, her paper name to Americans while she was either Lee Tai or Lau Tai (Mrs. Lau)O as my father's wife in Chinese; but she always identified herself as *Wong May Yee* (her maiden name) since this was who she was. She changed her American name to *Fung Gor Jung Lee or Fung Gor Lee* after my father died.

My father had even more names. Born as *Ben On*, he took on *Yew Ock* to mark his entry into adulthood. During his life, he kept both surnames of Lau and Lee out of respect and obligation to his birth and adopted parents. His paper name was *Kim Lau* while he chose *Louis Tong* as his first business name in America and *Louis Kim* when he ventured on to open a new laundry. He finally became *Kim Lau Lee* after he "confessed", complying with the Family Reunification Act of 1965; he kept this name until his death. If you add the different spellings to the Lau and Lee surnames because of different dialect pronunciations and changes made by immigration authorities upon entry in the United States, we can each claim to several more names.

My parents gave us all nicknames, a typical Chinese custom to mark a particular character trait. Out tenants who were often late in paying their rent were called, *heem do*, meaning "owe rent". My sister was called *gai na Ha*, meaning "hen Anna" for her spirited fights to protect her rights. Nicknames were not always complimentary as my father called me *pi gay por*, *or* "beggar woman" since I often did not fit standard size clothing because of my size.

What's in a name? Each is symbolic. It denotes our lineage; it marks our milestones; it denotes different parts of our identity. In Western culture, the emphasis on integration is paramount to our identity. In Chinese culture, there is not this need to bring it all together. After times of adversity, after major milestones, but most importantly because of contrasting world views, Chinese sometimes deem it best to keep the different aspects separate. Instead of pathologizing this splitting, perhaps we need to recognize how multiple selves can exist across multiple contexts—in our Chinese American identities.

PART II: AN INTERGENERATIONAL SAGA

As we examine Chinese mythology and contemporary storytelling, the themes mirror the life experiences of Chinese American immigrants. and capture the immigrant experience. Life is a journey and the immigration experience highlights a journey with added challenges of uprooting and transplanting to a new and different culture. It is the thesis of this book that as immigrants make this journey and tell their stories, they create new legends about the cycle of life to sustain them and nurture their children. These immigration legends become part of their group's identity. Each family creates its own immigration legend to preserve its history. This legend is communicated to future generations.

Part II of this book uses oral history to capture this story for a Chinese American family. This family saga describes an immigration journey and the influence of mythology and cultural symbols in its daily life. While this is a story of one family, all immigrant families might identify with the immigration themes of abandonment and loss, trauma and survival, guilt and obligation, and journey and rebirth. The bonds we create and the bondage from which we cannot escape are the challenges and trials of all immigrants, not unlike those made by Monkey King in his journey to the West.

The use of oral history captures the subjective experience and psychological dilemmas of the immigration experience. It shows defining moments—those transformative moments in our individual lives—that establish our cultural and self-identities. This section is told in my mother's voice to capture the anguish and joys of her experience—and that of Chinese American immigrants living in a bicultural environment. Some of these stories were retold many times by my parents during our childhood—

their purpose being to teach, to heal and to cope. The interaction between mother and daughter captures the bonds in this relationship.

A Study of Contrasts

What happens when an Asian American daughter achieves middle-class educational and economic status, and in doing so, attains a social standing never dreamed of by her immigrant mother? How does an Asian American daughter establish a mother-daughter bond when she cannot fathom the trauma of separation, abandonment, and death experienced by her immigrant mother because of war, poverty, and immigration? How does an Asian American immigrant mother adapt to the world in which her daughter lives and advise her of that which she has not experienced? As Chinese American women face the challenges of stereotypic images of Asian women, of surviving amidst cultures of poverty and racism, of coping with contrasting expectations from Western and Chinese cultures, they are the women warriors of today. They must fight the battle to assert their place while being perceived as modest or exotic. They must fight the battle to enter an arena that may be closed. As mothers and daughters, they share an emotional bond that can transcend generational differences. Together they can create the immigration legend that transforms the future.

While the differences between Western and Chinese cultures are significant, the plight of all Americans has been to make this journey and fight the battle, for there are few among us who can claim not to have descends from foreign shores, and struggled to be liberated on American soil.

The Sociopolitical Context

Fung Gor Lee was born in Hoiping, China in 1911, the year of the Republic of China under Sun Yat Sen; she died in 1994 at the age of 84 in New York City Chinatown. During her life, she moved from the village to Nanjing city, and immigrated to the United States in 1939 just before WWII. In 1949, the forming of the People's Republic of China under Mao-Tse Tung closed the bamboo curtain to the West and severed direct communication with her family in China. This was paralleled by McCarthyism in the United States promoting anti-Chinese and anti-communist sentiments, and restrictive immigration policies toward the Chinese. My mother lived through the Civil Rights Movement and Women's Movement of the 1960s which was paralleled by the Cultural Revolution in China beginning in 1966 when Mao Tse Tung called on the nation's youth to purge the "impure" elements of Chinese society and revive the revolutionary spirit of the civil war two decades earlier. She had the opportunity return to China after 34 years following President Nixon's trip in 1972, and finally reunited with her son after 50 years of separation under 1965 Family Reunification Act.

CHAPTER 4: SURVIVAL AND STRIVING

This intergenerational saga is about contrasts of culture—biculturalism, and of the immigration journey taken by my mother Fung Gor Lee. The bonds we felt as we connected with family and friends contrasts with the bondage of being trapped by circumstances from which we could not escape—discrimination, inequities. I began recording these stories by my mother when she was 70 up until her death at the age of 84. They are recorded in her voice spoken in Chinese; hence the grammar may appear unusual given the differences in grammatical and linguistic structure between English and Chinese. He words are in italics. The Romanized versions of Chinese words do not follow any formal translation system because there is none for the village dialect of Toisanese Chinese. The names follow the Chinese tradition of addressing parents, relatives and honored friends by honorific titles denoting their hierarchical rank and relationship in the family order. This is the proper order of things. The table below lists the honorific titles used by me to address the family and relatives described in this saga.

Table 1: Honorific Titles

Name	Honorific Title	Relationship to Author
Kim Lau Lee	Papa	Father
Lee Kok Nong		Mother's first born son
Lee Sel Ming	Ming Gor	Elder Brother
Fung Gor Lee	Mama	Mother's Paper Name
Wong Tung Guey	Dai Q	Eldest Maternal Uncle
Wong Mei Yee	Mama	Mother's Maiden Name
Wong Chun Hoy	Poy Q	Maternal Uncle Poy

Wong Hing	Hing Q	Maternal Uncle Hing
Wong Hing	Cheung Por	Maternal Great Aunt
Unknown	Ah Nerng	Maternal Great Stepmother
Wong Gim Hing	Ah Yee	Maternal Aunt
Wong Shee Chew	Ah Gung	Maternal Grandfather
Wong Fei Gong	Bul Gor	Maternal first cousin
Oliver Finds	Kai Gung aka Godfather	Maternal Grandfather-paper
Willie Lau	Ah Gor	Elder Brother
Anna Ong	Ah Jeer	Elder Sister
Scott Chin		Son
Stephin Chin		Son

In the Beginning: The Floods

According to the ancient Chinese myth, there was the Great Flood. After the waters subsided, Moon Goddess sent her representative to earth to re-people the world. This gave birth to all living things--a renewed world and a new creation. Men, women, and all animals arose from the different parts of her person. Not only is the Moon Goddess the life giver—creating all life on earth, but she is also the destroyer--this flood was her doing since she is the cause of rain and storms, and the tides. But she laments her consequences, and does her best to save her children (Harding, 1971, p.109).

After the floods, the Toisanese immigrants came to America. From tiny farming villages in the southern part of Canton Province in China came scores of peasants immigrating to the shores of the United States during the early 1900s. The floods of the Pearl River had devastated the land. Driven by the scourges of poverty, striving toward the fruits of prosperity, seeking to return as respected men to their families in China, they came in search of the Golden Mountain. The mountains of San Francisco gleamed with gold as they beckoned across oceans. Their shimmer behind the setting sun of the West embodied dreams from the East. They belied the darkness of the tunnels and railroads, of the sweat and toil that lay ahead.

With the Toisanese immigrants came their hopes for a life of splendor, reminiscent of emperors, a sure escape from the certainty of starvation. Alas, with them came their differences of culture and language, of values and lifestyles, which thrust them into a world of indifference, a sea of racism that kept them oceans apart from their neighbors next door. They came, separated from their homeland, leaving behind loved ones. They lived alienated from the mainstream, yearning to return home to China, illusions of what was to be; they survived in America.

In My Mother's Voice

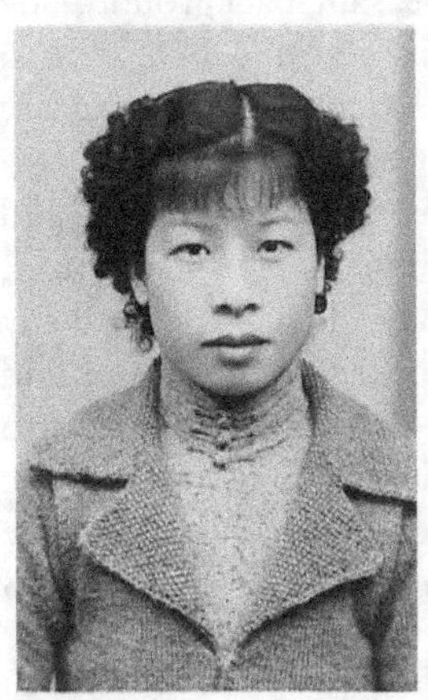

1 Fung Gor Lee - circa 1939

Through the voice of my Toisanese mother, we can hear the anguish; the anguish of loss, abandonment, and guilt. Through her eyes, we can see the world in its vastness separated by oceans, and yet so small in New York City's Chinatown of five long blocks along Mott Street with a one mile radius. My mother was Toisanese, an immigrant. As she aged, her voice grew loud as she lost her hearing in one ear and was reduced to 10% hearing in the other. Her voice cried out on ears too hurried to hear stories frozen in time and place while the world moved on. Her Chinese words struggled to reach English ears, unable or sometimes too arrogant to give them their due. Her world was confined by the limitations of her hearing; we would bemoan the isolation she must have felt. How much the alienation of cultures between East and West, or the need to preserve what she left behind left her content to close herself to the new worlds we now sought, we will never know. We do know how sometimes, her world, rich in imagination, drew upon the depth of her experience to make up for what she could not or chose not to hear. She was an active, and energetic woman till her death.

When I left my mother's home to follow my professional and personal pursuits, I left New York City where I was born and moved to Boston, a distance of 250 miles. For years, at the end of each of our visits together, my mother felt renewed anguish over the losses she had experienced so long ago. Separated by distance, and limited by the time we could spend together, my mother and I found our vacations together a time to bond. In our travels together, her hearing loss made it difficult to converse together especially in public places where her loudness would render me self-conscious although it did not bother her in the least. To pass the time, I often urged her to recall memories of her past, this became her saga. Since her hearing was so poor, I listened to her stories and recorded them on my computer. As I recorded, she spoke more fluently; both she and I felt her oral history would be for posterity—for our children and family.

This was different from my siblings who, in their frustrations, argued and yelled. They were always trying to get her to hear what they wanted to hear. The more they yelled, the less she heard. I merely listened to what she wanted to say. I heard the wisdom, and continuity of her simple words. I heard the anguish of her experience. She had been educated only till the sixth grade, which was average for girls in her time, but is limited by today's standards. Knowing this and modest about her peasant background, she was reticent to talk at first. But spurred by my interest and her wish to transmit and preserve our family history, she recounted and shared her view of the world. I recorded these memories for her, for us, for history.

My mother's story is a saga of contrasts, of immigration, of culture, and of poverty. Through her eyes, this saga speaks of intergenerational bonds, of mothers and daughters, and of survival and striving. It records what my mother believed, in her modesty and simplicity, to be too mundane and insignificant to be recorded. And yet, it is her voice that I hear, that calls to me, to remind me of her wisdom and of the limitless boundaries of the world today. It speaks to the impact of immigration, of poverty, of the sociopolitical context on the lives of immigrant families. This saga is told in her voice.

Memories of China—Family Obligation and Loss

The Sojourner (1890-1910)—Ah Gung's Pride and Determination

2 Ah Gung - MGF

With the California Gold Rush began the large immigration of Chinese to America. Many of the young men in Toisan went to gnoy yerng (overseas) to find their fortune. Gnoy yerng--that's what we called America. You never had to worry about having something to eat. Everyone was rich there. How we envied all those young men who would bring back gold and riches for their families.

(This was the immigration myth—as many Toisanese came to believe. California was the Golden Mountain of the West. It was the Melting Pot where everyone can follow their dream. It was a dream of things unimaginable.)

Ah Gung was no different. There were no opportunities left in Toisan. All we could do was farm; but the land was barren. The floods were frequent, washing out the rice fields from time to time. There was often nothing to eat since we depended on the land. People were dying. Beggars filled the streets. America beckoned to all of us. This was our hope. The passage from China to America took one month by boat; there was no plane travel in those days. People would get seasick since most had never even sat on a train or in a car. They would get dizzy, and unable to eat for the whole month waiting to get to America.

Ah Gung had saved barely enough money to make the passage; he was determined to become prosperous for our sake. People really did not know where they would end up, only that they were going to gnoy yerng. It was America, it was the land of the Golden Mountain. Ah Gung ended up in Vancouver working for the lo fan (Mr. Foreigner) in the gold mines. Lo fan, that's what we call white people. Chinese were not allowed to mine gold in those days, only to work for the gold miners. Chinese were not allowed any real status. We could only get the jobs nobody wanted. Once in America, we struggled to make ends meet. Sometimes the suffering was as bad as it was in Toisan. This was true for Ah Gung when he got to America, only we did not know it at the time.

The letters we got never said a word. Ah Gung was a proud man; he would never write to tell us how difficult it was or how hard he worked. Only when he returned to China did we learn how hard it had been; there were times when he did not from where his next meal would come. When he realized the opportunities in the gold mines were reserved only for white people, he tried his luck elsewhere. He was determined not to give up. He tried to open a restaurant but that failed after one year. Then, he opened a grocery store but that also failed.

Very little is known about what happened since Ah Gung was not one to tell us too much. We had to guess and piece together from the few things he would say. When he returned to China, he brought home gold dust worth about $800, not much even in those days. But he was a proud man; I never dared complain that this was all he had to show for the ten years he spent away from home. Ah Gung was a good father; he provided for the family. He was the Sojourner.

The Good Brother—Dai Q's Family Obligation

3 Ah Gung and Dai Q and my Mother circa 1937

I lost my mother when I was five. (This was how my mother always described her mother and her childhood. It was shrouded in mystery; yet, her pain and the loss was evident each time she repeated this.)

Poy Q's (maternal uncle Poy) parents took Dai Q (eldest maternal uncle) and me in. Dai Q was 15 and I was 5 at the time. Without my parents around, I had no one to protect me from the meanness of the other children. Poverty does strange things to people; people look down on you. Not having a mother, I was dern (pitiful). I would eye the other children enviously as their mothers would fend for them and hoard the best food for them. I would always talk about Ah Gung proudly to my friends to prove to them that I too had a parent who cared. I would say, "My father is in gnoy yerng (overseas), and is taking good care of us." He always sent money home so Poy

Q's parents would take good care of me. Along with it was always a letter telling us about what he was doing. From his letters, I imagined that the streets in America were paved with gold. I imagined that he was living the life of an emperor with servants at his beckon serving his every need. Privately, I cried myself to sleep many a night over not having a mother to watch over me. Little did I imagine how much Ah Gung had suffered. It was not until his later years back in China that he would lament, "Going out into the world to find one's fortune is a fate more pitiful than the life of a dog". (Dogs were eaten for food in China. Unlike in America where they are raised as pets, a dog's life was pitiful because one wrong turn and they were gone. This was why whenever our dog misbehaved, my mother would threaten to cook and eat him; we never did of course. My parents would only raise German Shepherds because they had a purpose as good watchdogs to protect the house.)

Ah Gung was a good brother. To repay Poy Q's father for taking care of me, he tried to help him get a new start. He gave his brother money to start a business. Besides, this was a must since it was his obligation as the eldest son. His advice to Poy Q was "Don't rely on people. You must work hard to make your own living. This way, you'll always be independent." Poy Q always remembers these words of advice, and tells me so to this day. Poy Q went on to start his business as a shirtmaker in Hong Kong. We always had this bond since we grew up together in the same household. Although we are first cousins, we are as close as any sister and brother. That's why I helped him to immigrate here to America.

(My mother had sponsored Poy Q and his family to the U.S. They arrived in the US in the 1980s after 40 years of separation. This practice was common among Toisanese immigrants to fulfill their obligation and debt to their families. A man's character is often judged by how he meets his family obligations)

Unfortunately, Poy Q's father was not so lucky. He "bought papers" twice trying to emigrate out of China. (This was how most Chinese immigrated during that time given the restrictive anti-Asian legislation in effect at the time. They assumed the identity of the papers they purchased often at astronomical prices, and at great personal and financial risk.)

The first "paper" expired because Poy Q's father needed to get surgery for his sa-gnon ("sandy eye"). (This was often how we understood medical problems. We were never sure if these diseases were based on medical fact, cultural folklore or merely poor translations. At the time, we would shrug it off as heresy since "we knew better; ". Now we wonder if this was cataract surgery.) *The second "paper" Poy Q's father bought limited his entry to Canada; he never made it there either. Ah Gung then gave money to Poy Q's father to help him emigrate to France. He felt it was Poy Q's father's turn now to go out in the world to find his fortune. First, Ah Gung gave him $500; later, he gave him another $300. That was a lot of money in those days. But Poy Q's father could not find a job in*

France; things are never as easy as our imagination would have us think. He could not make a go of it. Ah Gung finally sent money to Poy Q's father to help him return home to marry in China.

Ah Gung was a good man. He did all these things not expecting to be repaid; he just wanted to be appreciated. That is a virtue in our culture. That is why Poy Q treats me so good now; he is repaying his father's debt. He is very respectful; he always remembers. Poy Q will often come up to visit me and take me out for dim sum even though I don't eat very much. It is the gesture that counts. He never forgets my birthday; he always brings a chicken to honor me. (She sat back with a radiating smile as she pondered being so honored; I could hear the appreciation and pride in my mother's voice. It mirrored the smile of Ah Gung in the huge picture of him hanging high in our living room seemingly looking over us. These pictures always held a prominent position in many Chinese households)

Bearing the Irrevocable Losses (1911-1930)— Accepting Fate

I was the fifth and youngest of five children. Three of my siblings died; my sister died when she was seven. I had two brothers who died; one died when he was eight; the other when he was ten. That left just me and Dai Q who was ten years older than me. I lost my mother when I was five. Times were tough during those days in China. When people got sick, there was not the medicine to do anything about it. Many times, we did not even know what they died of. That's why we had so many rituals to protect us just in case there were evil spirits around wishing us ill will. On the other hand, maybe it is all in one's fate; a person's life is destined to follow a certain course. You can't change fate; you just have to accept it. (These stories of loss, abandonment and separation pervaded my mother's stories. She spoke of her multiple losses in a simple, matter-of-fact way. Yet, her unresolved grief was clear in her need to repeat them so frequently. My mother never got over the loss of her mother at age or her having to leave her 5 year old son in China. The mystery that shrouded my maternal grandmother was lifelong. When pressed, she would say, "Let's just say she died. I don't remember her".)

I was born July 23 in Men-Guo Year One (1911) in Hoiping, China in the village of Hen Gong. This is a village not far from Toisan where your father was born. (My mother, as did many Toisanese, often counted the years from the beginning of the Republic of China in 1911 as year one. I never really knew if my mother was born 1911 or 1912 since she practiced the Chinese custom of adding a year to her age on New Year's Day—making her one year old when she was in fact only 6 months. She also used the lunar calendar to calculate her birthday—meaning that her birthday was different each year based on the Gregorian solar calendar that we used. Adding further complexity, her "paper" age was 9 years younger than her birth age; often confusing us as to how old she really was—since Chinese liked to add years to their age to gain the respect and honor that comes with age.)

People stayed in their villages for life. That's why families "take in a daughter-in-law". When a woman leaves her village upon marriage, she lives in her husband's village for the rest of her life even if he dies because she now belongs to her husband's family.

When I was born, I was named Gim Slen (New Gold). When Gim Nul (Golden Daughter) my older sister died, I was renamed Tel Hai because my mother was afraid I too would die. They thought the old names were now bad omens. Hai means another younger brother will come soon. My parents were trying to change fate by renaming me; the words of my name are symbols of bringing new life. But I never liked this name because I lost my mother under this name. So when I turned 13, I took the name of Mei Yee (Beautiful Start) to symbolize a new start. Ah Gung, your grandfather, had returned from gnoy yerng (overseas) by then, and I wanted to start anew.

Ah Gung was 20 years old when Dai Q (Eldest maternal uncle) was born. He was 30 years old and was goldmining in Vancouver, Canada when I was born. By the time I was 5, I had no mother anymore. In July of that same year, Ah Gung's mother, my grandmother died. So I lost both my mother and grandmother when I was 5. Ah Gung wanted to make sure there was someone to take care of me. He wrote to Poy Q's father to ask him this favor. With the money from Ah Gung, Poy Q's father was now in a position to marry. He quickly married Cheung Por (Great maternal aunt) so that she could help Ah Gung raise me. (My mother described these events in a matter of fact manner because mortality was so commonplace in China--Life was dictated by pragmatics and economics. Decisions were often made for you by the elders. There was little choice in the affairs of marriage with decisions left to parents and matchmakers. (Her affect ranged from pain and anguish with a sense of resignation in her voice about life's experience and fate.)

Cherng Por resented being forced to raise me; she felt like a stepmother even though she was only my aunt. Poor her, I can't blame her! She was only 16 years old at the time she was forced to marry Poy Q's father. So, she took it out on me; she was mean and treated me very poorly. Sometimes, I would fall asleep on the floor because I had no mother to put me to bed. She would just leave me there; I was so dern (pitiful). Yet, Cherng Por would dote on her and spoil her own children, Poy Q and his sister. She carried him on her back until he was 3 while I had to fend for myself. Like my mother, Cherng Por had 6 children, 3 of whom died before Poy Q was born. I've forgiven her now. I honor her now that she is here in the United States.

Father and Daughter Bonds—1924

In Men-Guo 13 (1924 or 13th year of the Republic), Ah Gung returned to China from Vancouver. He was 43 now and had been away for 13 years. I was 13 that year when he remarried that September. Dai Q, my brother, was 23; he also married in November of that same year. This was the best and worst years of my life. I was still living in Hoiping when news arrived of Ah Gung's return home. On January 2, Men-Guo 14 (January 2, 1925) when I turned 14, I was told to accompany Dai Q and Dai Kim

(Eldest maternal aunt) his new wife, and Ah Por (Maternal grandmother) my new stepmother to join Ah Gung in Nanjing. I had never left the village before this, and Nanjing was cold (unlike the more temperate climate in Hoiping). I was thrilled that my father was coming home. I would now have someone to care for me.
The journey to Nanjing was long and hard. We lived in the city of GuangZhou for a few days, and then traveled for 7 days by boat to Shanghai. Ah Gung came out to Shanghai to pick us up at the designated meeting place. I was anxious and so excited. I had only seen him in pictures; I did not recognize him at first. When he arrived, I waited for Dai Q to introduce us; this was only proper since he was the elder brother. We politely acknowledged one another. (Protocol dictated that there were no teary reunions especially in public no matter how one felt.) *We proceeded on our journey together. We all stayed in a hotel for 2 nights, and then traveled for 4 hours from Shanghai to Nanjing. Next, we rode a "taxi" to BonKei, a suburb of Nanjing when we were to live.*

(This reunion of father and daughter was a defining moment embedded in my mother's memory. Every minute detail of the days preceding her reunion with Ah Gung was remembered; each moment was savored as a precious gem. This reunion at the vulnerable age of 13 was the culmination of years of pent up feelings since losing her mother at age 5. It demonstrated her father's concern for her welfare, his remembering her, and his keeping his promise to return and reunite the family after 13 years. Her father was a hero and protector, perhaps all the more necessary to counter her feelings of shame, anger, and loss of her mother at so young an age.)

Upon arrival to Nanjing, Ah Gung set about to build a house for his new wife. Alas, this marriage was short-lived. You see, my potential stepmother had a 7 year old daughter from a previous marriage whom she had brought with her to this marriage. This did not fit with Ah Gung's plan. He was concerned for our welfare. He intent to remarry was to reunite the family; he also had not told her that he was planning to return to Canada shortly. When the new wife found out his plan, she refused to stay in Nanjing alone, and ended the marriage. She returned the gold bracelets from the dowry to Ah Gung to compensate for the cost of the wedding banquet and expenses. Everyone was so poor in those days that this was considered only fair.

Ah Gung then went about to look for another wife because he wanted me to have a mother. Through a matchmaker, he finally remarried. Ah Nerng (Stepmother) was over 30 with two children from a previous marriage; her husband had been an opium addict. She did not have too many options; few men in those days were interested in women with this kind of history. They were considered tainted and immoral. Ah Gung refused to allow Ah Nerng to bring the 2 children (age 7 and 3) with her into our home because of me; he was always concerned for my welfare. (I wondered how my mother, always so nurturing and concerned about others, could be so unsympathetic to these children. I could only conclude that this preserved her view that her father's utmost concern was for her welfare. This was a common practice in China during those days when women depended on men for their livelihood; children from a previous marriage were a liability as they would have to share the already meager food and resources.) *Ah Nerng's former mother-in-law was angry when she found out about the marriage because she had expected Ah Nerng to remain in her household according to Chinese custom . Ah Nerng's former mother-in-law came looking for her for retribution. She hid while Poy Q paid her off with about $20 to get her to leave our house. Ah Gung and Ah Nerng had one daughter from this marriage; Ah Yee (Maternal aunt) named Gim Hing (Golden Sibling), who is 13 years younger than me, and is still lives in Nanjing.*

Ah Gung later returned to Canada once again to find his fortune, leaving me in the care of Ah Nerng. She was mean. She played favorites giving her own child Ah Yee, everything. I was resentful and jealous of her. When I would ask Ah Nerng for money to buy books, she would go straight to Ah Gung to complain; he would then scold me for being so greedy. You see, girls are not supposed to be greedy; if you ask for something, you are considered greedy. So Ah Nerng always knew how to manipulate the situation against me. Ah Yee always got the better of things; I got the leftovers. When I couldn't take it anymore, I cried to Ah Gung one day saying, I didn't think not having a mother would be so dern (pitiful). We then cried together commiserating over losing my mother. I always hated Ah Yee because I felt jealous of all the attention she got from Ah Nerng. She really is alright though. We write to each other now all the time.

Ah Nerng wanted to arrange to marry me off when I was only 14 so that she would be rid of me. Ah Gung refused because of his concern for me. He said it would be dern (pitiful) to marry me off so young. He accused Ah Nerng of being too-sum (heartless). He insisted that she raise me until at least age 18 or 19 before marriage. To prevent this from happening, Ah Gung asked the next door neighbor, Ah Seem to watch over me. (Following custom, good friends are often called Aunt-Ah Seem or Uncle-Ah Sook to bestow respect and intimacy to the relationship even though there was no blood relationship.) *Ah Gung made her promise to arrange a marriage only when I was of marrying age, and to help find a good man for me. He had the utmost concern for me.* (My mother spoke proudly of this as testimony to her father's utmost concern for her welfare. Long separations between husband and wife at the time were not uncommon as the men set out to find their fortune overseas.)

Arranged Marriage: Her Moral Character and His Trustworthiness

4 Fung Gor Lee, circa 1930s

In Men-Kuo 17 (1928), Papa came from gnoy-yerng (overseas) to Nanjing to find a wife. Our neighbor, Ah Sook (Uncle) met him one day and asked him if he was married. He told Papa that there was this Wong girl living next door to him who might be eligible for marriage; he was talking about me. He then told Papa, "Let me ask if she is willing. When she gets out of school, she always walks by and calls out to me. She is a good girl. She walks by here every day; you can take a look for yourself." Papa watched for me through this neighbor's window. When I walked by, he said OK, he was willing to marry me although he thought I was kind of small for my age; I am barely 4'10". Important characteristics for a good marriage in China were that a woman be of good moral character and a man be able to support a family. Papa and I were then formally introduced. We did not talk when we first met; I was shy and modest. Papa approved of this because he felt good girls should be shy. Ah Seem, the neighbor, gave me her opinion about Papa. She said he looked loh-seet (honest) and deung-tom (smart), but was concerned because he had a pei-hay (temper). My mother smiled at how Ah Seem was so gnon tom (had a sharp eye) for predicting my father's character. When I first saw Papa, I neither liked nor disliked him. (I wanted to know if it was love at first sight. I pressed her further in disbelief that she would consider marrying someone she did not know.) *All marriages are arranged. Whatever the elders said was OK with me; I was very obedient. Besides Ah Nerng was not good; she was mean to me. I felt I needed a mon-how (entrance or home) to go to. I was 17 years old by then and of marrying age. I cried that whole night because I felt I had no choice. It was a long and lonely night. I knew it was time to get married. I knew I would have to accept what the elders had decided. My fate had been decided, and I couldn't look back.*

Papa and I became engaged August 4, Men-Guo 17 (1928); we married on August 24, Men-Guo 17 (1928) when I was 17 years old. After we were married a month, I was y yeen (with child). Papa had built a new house in Nanjing for the family. We lived there together after the marriage for a year and 4 months. Papa then left again to go overseas, i.e., gnoy-yerng. As my father and uncle had done, I knew this was the way things were to be. I did not protest. Papa returned to Mexico on January 2, Men-Guo 19 (1930); I was 19 then and did not see him again for the next 9 years when I was 28 (1939). I tried to be patient and pass the time while I waited. I knew he would return and not abandon me.

Omen of The First Born Son

Did you know you had a brother who died? my mother suddenly asked. (I did not know this until I was well into adulthood. My mother had kept this secret for many years because it dredged up painful emotions of separation, guilt, and abandonment. Following Chinese custom, she counted him among her children. My mother's stories were sometimes confusing because of gaps in the dates. In my youth, I attributed these to her memory lapses or confusion of details. Only later was it clear that she was shielding from us that our brother Sel Ming in China was a replacement for this first brother.) *I gave birth to Kok Nong, my first son, on August 6, Men-Guo 18 (1929); he died August 21, Men-Guo 19 (1930) when he was only 1. Circumstances around his death were very strange indeed. He had not been sick. On that particular day, I had brought some food to a neighbor leaving him home. By the time I returned home, I found that he had fallen on the floor as if he was sick. We brought him to a Chinese Doctor who said he was not ill but could not tell us what was wrong. I did not know what to do, and wanted to put him in the hospital. I was persuaded by neighbors not to because they were afraid he would die there. I should not have listened because he died 16 days later. Hospitals are bad omens; people die there.*

After the fall, Kok Nong was fine during the day; but in the evening, he would cry all night as if the gul (demons) were disturbing him. I felt the gul caused him to die because he had not been sick. I then consulted a seen doctor (i.e., soothsayer) about him. The soothsayer prophesized that "Sitting in front of a door facing East, he met up with two gul-seen (demon spirits), a male and female spirit; the female was carrying the baby on her back." I tried to figure out what this meant. Our house sat with the front door facing East so this prophecy must have been referring to our house.

In fact, I had had a dream recently in which I saw two people I knew coming down by our house. Both these people had committed suicide so I knew this omen could not be a good one. One of these people was a Lee woman who had hung herself because her mother-in-law was no good and so terrible to her. In the dream, this woman said to me, "Tel, your child is so cute", and tried to reach out to touch him. Kok Nong started to cry in the dream. I awoke in a start and found him actually crying. I knew I had been carrying him sitting at the front door with several friends enjoying the breeze. This had to be a bad omen. The soothsayer also predicted that the baby would have only 3 more lives (meaning 3 more days left to live).

I found out later that at about the same time all this was happening, Papa had gone hunting in America and shot a goose. His friends had warned him not to do this since it was considered bad luck to kill a goose. Papa pooh-poohed their warnings saying he was not afraid. He always had a lot of guts. Kok Nong's death was probably retribution for what Papa did. (I was never sure if my mother really believed these omens, or whether they were consolation for events too painful to bear. She felt helpless and vulnerable and needed an explanation for this senseless death. It also was the basis for disagreements she and my father had for many years about my brother in China.)

The circumstances occurring up to Kok Nong's death was really strange; he was never really sick. After he fell, Kok Nong behaved very strangely (as if he was possessed). He would eat, but had no bowel movements. We watched over him for 16 days. On his last day, he tried to reach for me and called out "mama". I wanted so much to go to him. But the old women, the elders in the neighborhood who had gathered around ordered me to my bedroom; they told me not to answer him. They said the look in his eyes was not good. They were trying to prevent Kok Nong from dying; they believed that he would not leave to go to the next world if I, his mother, would not respond to his cry. I was in agony. I left the room as I was told hoping he would pull through, but he died anyway. (My mother spoke dispassionately. Though the passing years had done much to numb her pain, it was palpable and described as if it had happened to someone else. She paused and sighed.) *I remember him fondly; he was very smart. He was barely one, and could do so much. She smiled. When he saw people approaching, he would point them out to me. Do you know he looked like you? She then changed the subject.*

Journey to the West: Coming to America

The Long Wait to America (1930-1939)—Changing Fate

The wait for Papa was long. I tried to pass the time. World War II was soon to come. The Japanese had already begun to invade China. With these change of events, Papa decided that China was unsafe, and began to make plans for me to join him in America. I continued living alone in Nanjing until your Lau Ah Year (Lau paternal grandfather) invited me to visit GuangZhou village when I was 21. He was trying to use me as a pawn to get Papa to return to the Lau family.

Papa was born a Lau and adopted by the Lees. As the story goes Ah Yeen (paternal grandmother) was collecting chai (firewood) while she was pregnant with Papa. The stress from this induced premature labor. Lau Ah Yeen died during childbirth. Papa was the third of 3 sons who were 6 years old and 3 years old at the time. Papa came from a well-educated family and pedigreed background. Lau Ah Year was a teacher. The eldest son was later educated at Wong Poo Military Academy, a very reputable school in Toisan.

Papa was considered unlucky since his birth caused his mother's death. The Laus wanted to rid themselves of this fate. They already had two sons. When he was only 7 days old, Lau Ah Year wrapped Papa up and abandoned him. The Lee clan from a nearby village heard of this situation in the Lau clan. News spreads quickly. The Lees had three daughters, one of whom died recently at birth. Since everyone wants boys, the Lee clan decided to adopt Papa and bring him home so that he would receive the milk of Lee Ah Yeen (paternal grandmother) who was still nursing. The Lees planned to raise Dad as a replacement for the baby who died. When Papa was taken in, it was obvious he had been neglected; he was unwashed and had been soaking in his own feces for some time.

In the Lee family, Dad fate was changed; he was the favored child. He was spoiled rotten and honored because his entrance had changed the luck in the family. Two sons were born to Lee Ah Yeen after Papa entered the Lee clan. When Papa reached adulthood, Lau Ah Year had a change of heart. He regretted having given up your Papa for adoption. He now tried to get Papa to return to the Lau clan and to recognize him as father. Papa refused out of loyalty to his adoptive parents to whom he always remained indebted for raising him. However, he later agreed to call Lau Ah Year his godfather to acknowledge these biological ties. This did not stop Lau Ah Year from continuing to try to bribe Papa with gifts to win his affection and maintain the family lineage. In later years, Lau Ah Year would often invite Papa to the Lau clan celebrations. It was Lau Ah Year who gave Papa those 9 gold coins that he brought with him to the America. These were the coins I gave to you as a teenager. (I had brought them to a jeweler to make into a bracelet. When I went to pick it up, the jeweler showed it to me and dropped it into a bag behind the counter. Once outside the store, I was so excited, I opened the bag to see the bracelet. The bag was empty; I had been conned. I immediately returned to the store; the jeweler denied everything.) *My mother was extremely upset but felt helpless because she did not speak English. I was blamed for being so careless.*

I never thought much of your Lau Ah Year. I felt he was manipulative. On the other hand, the Lee clan was more virtuous. Lee Bahk Gung (Paternal Great Grandfather) was also a sojourner. He left for gnoy-yerng one month after his marriage. He lived in San Francisco working on the railroads. He returned to China decades later at the age of 61. He felt he had achieved his goal because he was able to buy 40 acres of land for the family. Lee Bahk Por (Paternal Great Grandmother) was 50 by the time he came home; consequently, there were no children from this union. Lee Bahk Por was angry with him because she felt her life had gone by. She chided him, "If you were home, we would have a houseful of children by now, and there would be people to work on the farm. Now we're old and there is nothing."

Lee Bahk Gung, on the other hand, felt there was no future in the village; he came back only for his retirement. This was typical of many of the early Chinese sojourners. He advised Papa to "Always carry $50 for security. Go live elsewhere. Don't come back to the village." His advice was instrumental to Papa's future; this is why he too went to gnoy-yeung. When he was ready to seek a wife, he went to Nanjing and found me. That's how fate brought us together.

Because there were no children from the Lee great-grandparents, your Lee Ah Year (Paternal Grandfather) was adopted along with his sister. Lee Ah Year did not like to work. Life was hard in the village so he decided to immigrate to Hawaii in 1910 when Papa was 6 years old. As I told you before, Papa had two older sisters. One was married. The other died a year after her marriage; she committed suicide because she was so unhappy in the marriage. Women didn't have choices in those days if their in-laws were no good. Suicide was often the only escape.

As I told you, Papa's entrance into the Lee clan brought two younger brothers, Ben Khin, your Sam Suk (Number Three Paternal Uncle), and Fook Ho, your Yee Suk (Number Two Paternal Uncle). He was originally named Ben Ho following Papa's name of Ben On. Shortly after he was born, however, someone by the same name in the village died so they changed his name to change his fate.

During the Japanese war, all your uncles and their families died of starvation. Ben Khin, your Sam Suk had a wife and two sons; they died during World War II from starvation. Fook Ho, your Yee Suk went to tend the buffalo; he was lucky because this meant he had a job which provided him with food to eat for a while. The Lee clan did not own any farmland so there was no food to eat when times got tough. This was particularly true during war or drought. Yee Suk died 2 years ago. He had a second wife and two children; they all also died of starvation. Of the nine, only the eldest son of Sam Suk named Ah Keung survived; he is still living in the village in Toisan. We sent him money to get married some time ago; he has one son and three daughters. I also sent money to his children, my great nephews, for them to get married. They asked for $600; I only sent $200 each. They are always asking for money. That was all I could afford since I am on Social Security; but the money goes a long way back in China. I don't know what happened to them now. (I sensed an apologetic tone in my mother's voice. My father's sense of obligation and debt continued through her while my mother's sense of resignation and acceptance was evident in her voice. While I recalled these names as a child when I overheard my parents arguing about their frequent requests for money, it was hard for me to keep track of all these relationships about uncles and cousins whom I had never met. It was to my great surprise in my visit to the Lee ancestral village in 2012 to meet my first cousins who I thought had all perished during WWII.)

A Man's Character and his Temper

Papa had a bad temper but a kind heart. (I remember my father as a tyrant with childhood scenes of him yelling at my mother. Yet, my mother's voice was matter-of-fact with a tone of affection.) *He was not afraid to die; he would fight with his life and confront any situation head-on. You remember when he would not let any of the laundry customers ha ba (intimidate) him. He would risk his life before he would let the lo faan (Mr. Foreigner) intimidate him. This was foolish at times, but he protected us and was proud. That was how he survived throughout life especially when he got to America.* (Her voice rose as she talked, conveying her respect for his behavior, though foolish, was protective and caring. I recalled stories from my childhood about how he would challenge racist and discriminatory behavior despite the risks and injustice the police and legal systems who were often unsupportive of the Chinese.)

He was defiant even as a child. There was a Hong Ah Bahk (Village Uncle) who was financially well off, but arrogant. You had to worry about these people in those days because they liked to push their weight around. He tried to ha-ba (intimidate) your Papa by belittling him, thinking Papa would be afraid of him. Papa fought with him instead. He went into this guy's house, took his wok and threw it on the floor to insult him. That was gutsy. He then stomped on and killed his chickens; you know how people treasured their means for food. Lee Ah Yeen was bearing Sam Suk at the time; Lee Ah Year had already died so she was already overburdened. When this Hong Ah Bahk came to complain about your Papa's behavior, Lee Ah Yeen was so distraught, she beat your Papa with a stick. Your Papa felt this was unjust; so he grabbed the stick used to stir the geesee gon (pigsty) and hit her back. Papa claims this was the only time Lee Ah Yeen had ever hit him. Papa was always proud of how fresh and defiant he was as a child. Papa always proudly described the time he was punished by being hung by his legs and arms from a tree. He was so stubborn that even this could not sway him; he refused to repent at all costs. (My mother's voice was one of pride and amusement as she smiled and laughed. I remember hearing my father tell these stories repeatedly as a child—that he did not tolerate anyone treating him unjustly, not even from his own mother. He considered this behavior a sign of his character and bravery. These acts of bravery reflected the frustration of his bondage as a laundryman in America.)

Since Lee Ah Year was in gnoy-yeung, other village uncles, Hong Ah Bahk (Village Uncles) would try to help Lee Ah Yeen raise Papa. They would watch over Papa, trying to teach him and provide him with male role models. It's always difficult when your father is not around to teach you. Another Hong Ah Bahk gave money for Papa to study kung-fu. He thought this would help to discipline him; Papa stopped misbehaving after this. In fact, he was Moi Goo's (Younger Paternal Aunt) father who we used to visit regularly. Did you know she was well educated in China? It's a tragic story. She was brilliant and well known for her scholarly calligraphy. Here in America, she was a laundrywoman like everyone else. She never could accept this fate, and tried unsuccessfully to start other businesses here. Her husband, Ah Cherng (Husband of Younger Paternal Aunt) did not support or understand her. She became frustrated and depressed. She often got forgetful as she would get lost in her daydreams and neglect her family and work.

By the way, Moi-Goo's father was a big wealthy lawyer who trained in Beijing. Did you know that he was murdered by an angry client who knew how to em-mak (acupressure). He had four tep-see (concubines); in those days, wealthy men had many tep-see to demonstrate their social status. Moi Goo was from the second mother while Set-Soon Dai-Goo (Set-Soon Eldest of the Younger Paternal Aunts) was from the first mother. His fourth tep-see (Number four concubine) was given to him as a gift in payment for legal services to become his servant. Because there were no children from this marriage, she was forced to leave the family. Women were property, and bearing children was important to a wife's status and honor in those days. It was the only way to guarantee one's place in the family. A wife was shamed, and could not hold her head up, if she could not bear children—women's bondage. People were poor and there were no choices. (My mother spoke of an era so incomprehensible to me that it led me to ponder the challenges she faced during a time when poverty and restricted social boundaries prevented women from gaining the independence that is possible today.)

Yee-Moon Suk was another Lee Hong Ah Sook (Village Uncle) who ended up in New York City. We used to visit him regularly as well. He had a reputation for siding with the winning side whichever it was--described as tul-fung (blows with the wind) by those who knew him. He lacked integrity. He sided with the Japanese when they invaded and occupied China. Later, when the Communists overruled China, he switched sides again. Character is important to a man. One must stand up to one's beliefs even if it means suffering the consequences.

A Woman's Honor and her Virtue

I visited Toisan village in GuangZhou when I was 21 at the beckoning of your Lau Ah Year. I had nothing to do; I was biding my time while I waited for your Papa to return. It was already four years. The visit to Toisan village was an unpleasant experience so I was anxious to return to Nanjing after a year; I was 22 by then. While I was in Toisan, your Lau Ah Year wrote a letter to Papa telling him that I was frivolous. He was trying to force me to stay in the village so he could always reach Papa for money. I was furious with him for trying to tarnish my character by attacking my virtue; I have not forgiven him to this day.

This caused trouble between Papa and me because good women are not supposed to be frivolous; it is a sign of bad character to be wanting excitement and spending money. Lau Ah Year's letter declared that I was moe-sam goo-ga (lacking interest in tending to the family). Papa was concerned that I lacked character and wrote to Yee-Bahk (Number Two Elder Paternal Uncle). Yee-Bahk tried to help; he brought the letter to Lau Ah Year and confronted him. In trying to support me, he defied his father, and ended up in an argument with him. Lau Ah Year was angry at this accusation by his own son; he smacked him for being so disrespectful. Do you know what Lau Ah Year then did? He took away all the money Papa had sent to me to prevent me from leaving GuangZhou. I felt imprisoned and trapped in GuangZhou. I was worried that I would never be able to get out of Toisan village.

In desperation, I wrote to Papa and appealed to him to send money to Dai Q to help me leave. I wrote to Dai Q to ask for his help; I asked him to come get me, and take me back to BonKei, Nanjing. I finally was able to leave. When I returned to Nanjing, I decided to resume school because I had nothing to do. I was still waiting for your Papa; I finished grade 6. (This attack on my mother's honor was an assault to her character and virtue, and was considered unconscionable. My mother's anger lasted 60 years and resurfaced when we met members of the Lau clan on a trip to Los Angeles.)

Replacing a Son—The Adoption

5 My mother and Sel Ming, circa 1930s

When I was 23, I adopted Sel Ming, your brother; he was 7 months born in October or November. His mother had been a poor farmer. The family had nothing to eat except a few morsels of bread and jook (congee). He was so pitiful when I first took him in. His clothes were all patched and worn; even the patches were patched. Sel-Ming's mother needed money for food to feed the rest of the family so they would not starve. She decided to sell Sel Ming since he was the third child. This was common practice then; it was the only choice when you were poor. Noone wanted him because he was so small; they figured he was unhealthy. She asked me to adopt him, begging on her knees for me to take Sel-Ming to give him a chance for survival. She bared her breast to me to show how her nipples had been bitten sore from nursing because she had no milk. She cried profusely, and was so desperate she was even going to just leave Sel Ming there. All the relatives urged me to take him; they took pity on her. The poor woman was asking $40 for him. When we finally agreed to the deal, the broker took $20 for his expenses leaving the poor woman with only $20 for herself. I took pity on her as she cried and gave her an extra $20.

For the next five years, Sel Ming and I lived in Nanjing waiting to hear from your Papa. It was nice to be raising a child again. It kept me busy, and we spent some pleasant times together. I preferred this less rigid life in Nanjing city compared to the small mindedness of Toisan vlllage. World World II and communism was soon to change this pace of waiting and watching the passing of life.

Escape from the Rape of Nanjing (1937)

Then World War II started. It was a nasty war. The Japanese invaded Shanghai on July 7, Men-Guo 26 (1937) and were heading for Nanjing. When the news broke, we were afraid. We prepared to flee our home and head for Hong Kong. We rushed to escape since we heard stories of atrocities committed by the Japanese soldiers; civilians including women and children were tortured and killed leaving no survivors. There were stories of women first being raped, and then slit with a sword right up the middle. This was a most difficult and traumatic time for me. From Nanjing, we had to reach a boat in GuangZhou in order to make the passage to Hong Kong. This was over 1,000 miles; transportation was poor in those days. The whole city was in chaos; there were people fleeing from all over. Some people walked for 7 days straight to get there and were exhausted. Others, not used to the city, had come down from the mountains and were bewildered.

We fled Nanjing by train to get to GuangZhou. I was carrying Sel Ming on my back. I carried only one bag with a change of underwear; we had to leave most of our belongings because we could not carry them. First, we rode a fire-car (train) for two whole days from Nanjing to Mo-Wu. Our whole family left together including Dai Q, Sel Ming, Ah Gung, Ah Por, Poy Q, and Hing Q. For three days and nights, we rode the train. The train was packed with standing room only. There was no place to sit; there was no place to move. We had to sleep standing up. It was a long and strenuous trip. I carried Sel Ming on my back during this entire trip. I was exhausted and weak. After two days of riding like this, a soldier sitting in front of me took pity on me and told me to sit on his lap. There was no place to move or he would have given me his seat. He assured me not to worry about his intentions, and insisted that I sit. I finally complied (not worrying about improprieties) because I was so tired.

There was no food or toilets on the train. All I had with me for food was a thermos of water and some soda crackers; that did not last very long. Everyone did his or her daily functions standing up; there was no place to go. We all tolerated the stench from one another. Several women were in the advanced stages of pregnancy. When they were due to deliver, the people standing nearby tried to move aside to make some room. The poor women had to give birth standing up. As for me, I began menstruating at some point during the trip; I was unable to change or clean myself up, I was soaked in blood. I was embarrassed but you can't think about it during times like that. We were all exhausted. But, we dared not complain; we were frightened that the Japanese would overtake us and just felt lucky enough to be able to escape.

The train stopped at Cherng-Sa for a rest. People were afraid to get off the train for fear that they could not get back on. Local residents came to the side of the train to sell us rice. Most of us hungrily grabbed for these limited morsels since we had not eaten for two days. One person had not finished eating when the train began to leave the station, and still had the rice bowl. The lady who sold the rice became frantic trying to get her bowl back; being poor, she was afraid she would be out a bowl. Others on the train took pity on her. Finally, someone threw some money out of the window as the train was pulling away to pay for the bowl.

We were finally able to rest at Nam-Hung after traveling for four days before starting out again on a boat for Hong Kong. It was crowded at the pier where the boat was docked. Everyone was frantic and anxious; they were afraid they would not get on. We waited on the pier all day from 6PM to 6AM the next morning so as not to lose our place in line. There was only one gangway and a mass of humanity struggling to reach safety. Everyone was fighting to board the boat; we had to use each other as a human ladder to get onboard. We climbed up from the pier through a porthole because we could not reach the gangway. There were 30 of us who fled from Nanjing including Poy Q, Hing Q, Dai Q and his family, Ah Gung, Ah Por, the Yeps and the Louies. Again the boat was packed. Seven of us had to sleep on one bed. There was no place to sit.

We had to stand all night again until the boat arrived in Horn-How. That's why those of us who made it to America are so close. (Suddenly, I realized the significance of these people in our lives growing up. The bonds that my mother made with them as they fled from Nanjing together were lifelong—spanning continents and reuniting after almost 40 years. They were mere strangers and relatives to us, but the depth of their bonds with each other were unfathomable.)

Those of us from Nanjing were on the first boat out of Nam-Hung. When the boat returned to pick up a second load of passengers, it was bombed and destroyed by the Japanese. There were no survivors. News was slow and not always accurate during those days. When news reached America that a boat had been bombed, Papa thought I had been killed. He moaned that "all was lost" and was in despair until he received my letter several weeks later that I was safe in Hong Kong. In Hong Kong, we heard that the Japanese invaded Nanjing the day after we left, and had pillaged the village. We were thankful that we were lucky enough to escape in time. That's why I have such strong feelings about the Japanese to this day.

(The Rape of Nanking refers to the almost unbelievable orgy of violence unleashed over several months by the Japanese army after it occupied Nanking, the capital of Nationalist China, in December 1937. There is dispute about the death toll, but most serious scholars place it in the hundreds of thousands. Chinese men were forced at gunpoint to rape their mothers and daughters. Japanese soldiers gang-raped women by the tens of thousands. They nailed women to trees. They drove stakes through their vaginas. They bound the hands of Chinese men, lined them up in long rows, and machine-gunned them into huge burial ditches. They bayoneted babies in front of their mothers. They buried people alive. Soldiers had "killing contests" and boasted to Japanese reporters of their scores. The Nanking atrocities were well publicized throughout the world at the time, and are usually mentioned in the standard Western histories of World War II. The memory of the rape of Nanking remains very much alive, it was not until 1985 that the government permitted a museum of the atrocities to be built there, and it has repeatedly prohibited demonstrations against visiting Japanese(Chang, 1997). My mother could never forget the pain, the trauma, but mostly the shame, at their defenselessness.)

CHAPTER 5: CHINESE WOMEN AND FAMILIES

My mother would remember and retell countless stories to us as did my father. Each time a story was retold, it was told as if it were the first time. As children, we were impatient and restless. We dismissed these as the musings of adults who lived in the past with nothing better to do. As children, we had better things to do; we wanted to play. As my mother told these stories, there was always pride mixed with reminiscing. She always seemed to be teaching us something. As adults, these stories took on new meaning as we saw them through her eyes—they marked her fate, told about her journey, and were attempts to heal. But the deep pain always remained, and could not be consoled. My mother's voice continues.

American The Melting Pot: The Immigration Myth

We all wanted to come to America. The stories we heard sounded like paradise. We all expected so much. We expected the streets to be paved with gold. Our stomachs would be full. We would never go wanting. All we had to do was work. Little did we know how hard that was to be, and that we would all be working in a laundry. The hours would be long; the days endless. We would feel different in a land where differences are not supposed to matter. Little did we think how much we would miss what we left behind, and long for the beauty and culture and essence of China. Back in the village, we used to pick lychees and other fruit off the trees. Family was always nearby; we felt safe since our neighbors all watched over one another. The passage of the oceans between China and

America separated and bonded us through the letters we wrote and the stories we told about the Golden Mountain of the West. Many were exaggerated and distorted to make the unbearable bearable and to preserve the connections we needed—we created these legends of fortune. More importantly, we could not lose face (shame) and could not bring ourselves to describe the squalid conditions under which we lived here in America. We needed to have face (pride); we maintained our loyalty and our family obligations, and continued to send money back home to our families in Toisan from the meager earnings of a laundry.

Abandonment and the Promise (1939)

After arriving safely In Hong Kong, I stayed with Poy Q, Hing Q, and Dai Q's family and made plans to join Papa in America. He had promised he would send for me. It was now almost 10 years, but I knew he would not abandon me. Papa had to buy papers to get me into the country since Chinese were not legally allowed to immigrate here given the quotas and anti-Chinese legislation in effect at the time. Papa had intended to return to China with a fortune as all the early Chinese immigrants before him did; but the war prevented that from happening now. The only papers he could find which would fit my description were that of a citizen's daughter; this meant that I could not be married or have a child. I was devastated when I found this out. I agonized over this because I knew it meant I would have to leave Sel Ming behind; he was only 5 at the time. I didn't know how to handle this so I took the advice of the elders and did not tell him.

But children know better. Sel Ming knew that I was planning to leave without him, and insisted, "I want to go with my mother to America. If they don't let me through, I will sneak under the turnstile." I didn't know what to say to him. I only knew I could not take him with me. I couldn't bring myself to tell him the truth. He would be staying with Dai Q. I didn't know when we would be together again. All I could do was to give him my last piece of motherly advice. So I told Sel Ming, "You be good. Stay with Dai Q, Dai Kim, and Ah Por. They will take care of you. When I get to America, I will bring you over". I never forgot my promise to Sel Ming. Papa and I frequently argued about this. China and America were changing; the immigration laws changed. I kept this hope alive that one day, Sel Ming and I would be reunited. The Family Reunification Act of 1965 made it possible. In 1976 after Papa died, I asked Willie (my brother) to initiate legal proceedings to bring Sel Ming over. (My mother and Sel Ming were finally reunited in 1989, 50 years after their separation; by then, he was a grandfather.)

When it was time for me to leave, it was the feeling of the elders that it was better for me not to say goodbye because Sel Ming would be too upset. I woke up early that day to get ready while he was still sleeping. I packed a bag; there was little of value to bring. I was amazed how little this was compared to the vastness of the people and memories I was leaving behind. When Sel Ming woke up, Hing Q took him out to play to distract him. I then stole out with Dai Q who brought me to the boat en route to America. No one could deal with the separation. I was later told that when Sel Ming returned from playing and found out that I was gone, he became frantic. He cried in desperation and ran to the pier trying to catch up with me. He was depressed for quite a while after that.

Dai Kim raised him for me just as Cherng Por raised me after I lost my mother and Ah Gung left for gnoy yerng. Sel Ming lived with Dai Q and his family in Hong Kong for several years until they returned to Shanghai after the end of World War II to open a shirtmaking business. Dai Q later opened a department store in Nanjing; he was not successful and lost a lot of money.

(At this point, my mother became pensive as if reliving once again the separation and abandonment of her son. I knew she was thinking how pitiful it was for him to grow up without a mother there to protect him. The pain in my mother's face was palpitating, but she had resigned herself to a fate over which she had no control. As a child, I remember her crying whenever she spoke of this, but I could never fathom the depth of her pain. She would never admit to her feelings of guilt because it would have meant she could have done something about it. And so, there were unspoken words between us as she and I bonded in our silence. With a shrug, she said,) *"Life goes in cycles"--what goes around, comes around.*

Angel Island and the Mexican Border (1939-1955)

6 My Parents, circa 1940

I arrived in America on January 5, 1939, from Hong Kong. The trip by boat took 18 days. We docked at Vancouver, Canada. I had a brief reunion with Ah Gung there and went onto Montreal. When I saw my father, I addressed him, "Pa". He then acknowledged me. We then spent a little time together. We were formal and cordial although the years of anguish still stirred inside. We each needed to maintain our dignity. I was now a grown woman, and going on to start a new life. This was to be the last time I would ever see him.

From there, I took another boat to San Francisco where I was detained on Angel Island for 3 months. It was ironic; I arrived there on Lunar New Year's Eve, a time we would have been celebrating and dining with family had I been back in China. It was one of the most depressing 3 months of my life on Angel Island; it was like being in prison. We were locked in our rooms, and had no freedom while we waited to be released. One of the interpreters took pity on us and tried to cheer us up at this detention center; he brought us chicken to celebrate the new year. I was petrified during my whole time there. I was afraid I would never get out of there. Periodically, the immigration authorities would take one of us into a room for interrogation about minute details of our lives. They would ask questions like: "Describe the room in which your father lived in China? Was the bed on the left or the right?"

All the questions were attempts to poke holes in our stories and catch us. We were in a hostile environment and were all afraid we would be caught lying and deported. This was the irony of my first taste of freedom in America.

On May 1, 1939, I finally received permission to leave Angel Island, and went to meet Papa in Boston. This was the point of entry. I was so relieved. Since Papa and I weren't supposed to be married, we got married once again to follow Western custom. We stayed in Boston for a week as a pseudo-honeymoon. Oliver Finds, my "paper father" was there to be witness at the ceremony. We even had another Chinese wedding banquet of three tables. We wanted to follow all the proper ceremony. The lo faan (whites) there wondered why we were treating this in so matter of fact manner, thinking we Chinese were just unemotional. They didn't realize we were already married and had a child together. (My mother was amused by the fuss the *lo faan* made over this Western style "wedding"; she accommodate them, but it simply did not have the meaning of her "real" wedding in China.)

From Boston, I went with Papa to New York to work in the laundry. It was only now, 11 years after my marriage that I first began to know the man I married. I learned that Papa left China on January 12, 1919 to come to Mexico to work as a farmer when he was 17. Since it was illegal to work until age 18, he added a year to his age in order to get work. Papa returned to China when he was 26 and married me when he was 27. After he left me, he wrote regularly. He told me he was going to America from Mexico. Whenever he wrote, I imagined all sorts of things. It seemed so simple, like a storybook. I couldn't really understand the magnitude of the difficulties and the dangers he faced, or the extent of the poverty he endured until I got here.

He came illegally into America in Men-Guo 21 (1932) under the assumed identity of a Lau; the papers he bought also happened to be his birth surname. Prior to leaving Mexico, he was afraid he would not make it to America so he made preparations in case he failed. He sent me $500 to put in the bank for safe keeping. If he made it to the America, he would send for me and this money was to be given to Dai Q to raise Sel Ming. If he was deported, the money was to be used for him to start a business when he returned to China. As fate would have it, he made it.

According to Papa, there was just a barbed wire separating America from Mexico. He entered through Mississippi lying under the boxcar of a truck to escape detection. The compartment was just small enough to fit a person; it had a cover on top like a coffin. It was a terrifying ordeal since he would have been shot if caught. There was another person traveling with him who died, apparently frightened to death. Papa was dai om (had a lot of gall); he was not afraid of anything. There was a Lo Lee (Mr. Lee) who picked him up in a limousine on the America side. The passage into America cost $10,000, a lot of money in those days.

After arriving in America, Papa had to go undercover and hid in the On Leong clan association for three days. We went through a lot of difficulty and danger to just get a decent living in those days. Papa worked for a while in San Francisco as a dishwasher. Forn Sook (Uncle Forn) was returning to China and had recommended Papa for a job in Woo Ming Doon, Nor Ga Lon (Wilmington, North Carolina) on a vegetable farm; he worked there for about one year until it closed. That was how we got jobs in those days—through introduction. Papa then came to New York in Men-Guo 22 (1933) because he heard that there were many Chinese there. Upon arrival, he found work in a laundry on Myrtle Avenue in Brooklyn; that was the only kind of work Chinese could do then. It was work no one else wanted. You have to smell the foul odors of people. You were treated with no respect by the customers.

Papa finally saved enough money to buy a laundry of his own for $300 on Marcy Avenue, Brooklyn. This was everyone's dream at the time, to have one's own business even if it was only a laundry. Times were tough then; it was during the Great Depression in America; the Japanese were at war with China in Shanghai. Papa ended up sleeping on an ironing board in the laundry because he was too poor to buy a bed. (This explained why my mother was so upset when we built a platform bed early in my marriage—she would bemoan how I had no bed to sleep in.) *When there was no business, he had no food to eat. Even so, he would send money back twice a year to support me; $200 at end of the year; $100 at midyear. This was enough to take care of me since expenses are so much lower in China. Life was not easy working in a laundry; I never realized how difficult it was until I got here. Customers taunt and disrespect you because you are Chinese. You have to tolerate it because there are no other choices for us to make a living.*

Since Papa came to America under the paper name of Lau, he connected with Cher Long Fong, the Lau clan association in New York City. They befriended him as a relative and helped him get started. These family associations were safe havens for newcomers and provided financial and other social services on an informal basis. Papa was grateful for this help, but was too proud to ask for continuing help; besides everyone else was going through the same. (We considered them family and visited the *fong* weekly on our Sunday outings to Chinatown during my childhood.) *But Papa, as you know, always wanted us to keep it a secret that we maintained our associations with our Lee clan as well. He was afraid that he would be viewed as disloyal.* (So we led double lives as both Lees and Laus.)

Born in America: The Impossible Dream (1941-44)

Papa and I toiled in the laundry on Marcy Avenue for several years. He always believed spirits lived there. He claimed that he often saw two children sitting and swinging their legs in the back room. Whenever he went back there, they would disappear. We ignored these spirits at first not knowing if they were good or evil spirits. Soon I was pregnant; but I miscarried when I was 4 months pregnant; this was before Ah Gor (Elder Brother) was born. I remember well the day I miscarried; Papa was not there. I had been standing on my feet all day ironing and working too hard in the laundry. Papa was visiting Mon Hong Bahk (Uncle Mon Hong) and returned home late. My stomach had been hurting all day, but I felt I had to keep going because there was so much work to be done. When Papa got home, he called a doctor who examined me and gave me some medicine to

prevent a miscarriage; I miscarried anyway. My legs began hurting so bad that I couldn't walk.

Ah Gor, (Elder Brother) was born in 1941, the year of the snake, just as World War II broke out. These were trying times; we were still living in the Marcy Avenue laundry. He had to suffer more because he was the first born. We were so busy working, we had little time for him. You and your sister were lucky; you did not ever have to sleep in a laundry. There were many strange happenings there. Ah Gor would wake in the middle of the night crying. Papa believed the spirits in the laundry were causing this so he decided to rent an apartment

7 Willie, Anna, Jean, circa 1940s

around the corner on Park Avenue to get away from them. Papa found that sometimes if you dropped a laundry ticket on the floor, it would come to rest standing up. Papa believed a spirit was holding it up. Even when there was wind blowing on the laundry ticket, it would not fall. This was ho kay qwai (so strange indeed)! Sometimes we would lose a laundry ticket. Neither of us knew where it went; it would just disappear. Later, the ticket would show up again in the same place. Papa felt the spirit had hidden the ticket and returned it. Why? I don't know.

Papa had been warned of these strange stories by the previous owner. At first, he did not believe them until it happened to him. He would hear strange noises which he felt must have come from those spirits. Spirits are known to haunt a place where there has been unrest from some experience in their lives, usually some kind of trauma or feeling of injustice. We could never figure out who this spirit was.

Ah Jeer (Elder Sister) was born the next year in 1942, the year of the Horse. Ah Jeer is the caring one; she is always so thoughtful. I remember her watching me stir the coals and ashes of the heating stove in our Marcy Avenue apartment. My face was black from the ashes; my brow sweaty from the effort. I'll never forget what she told me. She said she would hire me a servant when she grows up so I would not have to work so hard. This was enough to sustain my energy for years to come.

You were born 1944, the year of the Monkey, as the war was coming to an end. You were born in the evening at 12:45 AM at Columbus Hospital, a Catholic hospital. You were all Catholic. The nuns there were very nice. I did not want the pregnancy because life in America was so difficult. While I was pregnant with you, I would have Ah Jeer bounce on my stomach to try to initiate a miscarrriage. I fear that was responsible for the birth defect on your lip. We went through years of surgery and huge medical bills; your health was weak. This must have been my punishment.

We lived in a poor area and did the best we could. When you were one year old, you were crying terribly one night in your crib. Papa was furious at having his sleep disturbed; you know how bad his temper was. He also could never forgive you for those huge medical bills; you know how he was about money. I was worried because of the threats he was making and tried to calm you down, thinking you were just being temperamental. It was not until morning that we discovered that a rat had bitten your thumb and there was blood all over the crib. We felt terrible then. You still have the scar to show for it.

Ah Gung died February 1950 in Nanjing from an earache; he was in his 70s. This was very sad for me; I was not able to be there when he died. I was told that he was not feeling well and went to sleep. In his sleep, he fell off the bed. Dai Kim was making jook (congee) for him when the grandchildren went in and found him. He had been in a good disposition the night before so I don't know why it happened. Ah Por had died earlier that year. I used to get earaches; I fear my hearing loss is hereditary. When you were young, Papa used a home remedy trying to heal my earache; this caused my permanent hearing loss. He was dai om (audacious); he heard vinegar was a remedy for earaches and poured it down my ear one day; I felt a shiver and lost the hearing in my left ear after that.

I sometimes blame Boon Moo (Paternal Elder Aunt Boon) for Ah Gung's death. Shortly before Ah Gung's death, we had attended a funeral together. Upon returning from the cemetery, Boon Moo called me to look back at something. It is bad luck to look back when leaving a cemetery. I was hesitant but she urged me; regretfully, I turn to look back; a week later, Ah Gung died. Therefore, remember; you must "Never look back".

This was the end of an era. All of you children do not have to worry anymore; you cannot be deported. We were always afraid that we would be caught and deported to China. Now I am a 70 something year old woman; I am not afraid anymore. I have children and grandchildren "Born in America." My impossible dream has come true. They can't make me go back.

Defining Moments: Finding my Voice

Like my mother, I too found my voice. While our contexts differed, much is strikingly the same. Like my mother, there are memories that are etched in my mind that I remember across time and space; these are defining moments that capture the essence of the moment and the experience of a lifetime. My voice expands hers so that there is newfound strength as we echo one another.

I remembered the day my mother received the letter of Ah Gung's death. It was almost a month afterwards; but it was her moment to mourn. She sent Ah Jeer to pick me up early from school so that we could grieve together. I was only 6 at the time; I felt little emotion not having known my grandfather. But we all felt the distress and pain as my mother cried over her loss and her inability to be by her father's side at the time of his death. All the pain in her life gushed forth as the final loss of her father forced her to re-experience her losses once again. Her feelings of abandoning and being abandoned poured forth; she remembered losing her mother at age 5, her father's absence growing up, her leaving China and abandoning her family and leaving her son Sel Ming behind. We were too young to appreciate her pain; but we complied with her request to put pink yarn in our hair for the next week to show that we were in mourning.

We lived in Bedford-Stuyvesant, Brooklyn in a poor neighborhood with no other Asian faces. We felt an affinity with the one Filipino family there because we looked similar. Those were so few Chinese in America that my mother would become so excited whenever she saw an Asian face on the street; she would rush up to them and start a conversation with them in Chinese. Her questions were standard: "Are you Chinese? What is your family name? What village in China are you from?" If they responded, she would proceed to engage them in a conversation as if she had found a long lost friend. As children, we would cringe in embarrassment; but my mother paid us no heed. The isolation my mother felt was so overwhelming she threw all caution to the wind.

My memories are of the long and neverending hours of my parents working in the hot, sweaty laundry late into the night with the blinds drawn so as not to draw attention. They are of the Sunday family trips to Chinatown to connect with family members, whose true relationship were no more than distant relatives. Our extended family and cultural practices made everyone a relative, uncle, aunt, or cousin. Sunday was the only day of rest for my parents, and Chinatown was their only haven from the strange and seemingly unfriendly environment of Brooklyn. As we became teenagers, time seemed endless as we loitered on the streets of Chinatown on a Sunday afternoon. We belonged there; we stared at the tourists as objects of curiosity just as they did of us. These stories embellish those of my mother. They show our journey and the transformation that occurred as, together, we created our legend for our children and grandchildren.

Chinese Hand Laundry –*Slaving Away*

We owned a hand laundry as most Chinese Americans did in those days. It was called the Louis Tong Hand Laundry. Many of the customers called my father Louie thinking this was his name; he always greeted them in return and never corrected them. My parents worked together in the laundry during the early years of my childhood. Everything was done by hand in those days without the washers and dryers of today that led to the demise of hand laundries. My parents sorted the clothes, and then sent them to the Wet Wash. Shirts needed to be hand starched and ironed. There was standard way to iron and fold the shirts before they were stacked

and sorted for wrapping. The wrapped packages would be sorted by ticket number and stored on shelves for easy retrieval. As children, we helped with the wrapping, the cleanest and easiest part of the job. My parents reserved the smelly, more difficult part of the jobs for themselves. They were thankful for our help, but always afraid it would interfere with our studies. When business was good, my parents worked from 8AM to 10PM with little or no break. They dared not complain for fear of the lean times.

Sometimes there were customers set on creating trouble. They would make a false claim that we had ruined their shirts and insist on our paying for damages. With little command of English and a belief that Chinese could never win a case in the legal system, my parents often felt demoralized by these experiences and sometimes physically threatened. The settlement was often unjust in my parents' eyes, but was made to avoid further litigation or threat. It was clear that the lo faan (Mr. Foreigner or whites) wanted to make sure we knew our place; the message was that no Chinese would get the better of them.

The cash register we had in the laundry was a simple wooden box under the ironing board. In order to open it, you had to pull three of the five levers underneath simultaneously. If you pulled the wrong ones, it would sound a musical note, but not open, alerting my parents to unauthorized entry. This was installed to prevent burglaries; my mother was hard of hearing and probably could not hear it ring; but it made her feel secure. Sometimes I would quietly open it while my mother was in the back room. I would pick out the coins that I thought would be less likely to be noticed and run out to buy candy. I made up a ritual so as not to feel guilty. Since we did not get an allowance as our white friends did, I felt justified in doing this.

Beebee Gow (Baby Dog) was the dog we had in the laundry, a lovable energetic mutt. My parents could never admit that they wanted a pet (it was too much of a luxury for poor Chinese immigrants) so they justified his presence as "raising a dog to watch over the house." Though we had many dogs, we never bought any of them. *Beebee Gow* was inherited from my brother's godfather. When we took him in, we hated his name. We always tried to change it to no avail. We would call him *Prince, King, or Beauty*, names that we thought was more fitting for a dog. He would ignore our beckoning him, preferring to lie there looking at us. As soon as we called *Beebee Gow*, he immediately got up and came to us. We finally gave up, and he remained *Beebee Gow* for the rest of his life.

Beebee Gow was a free spirit; he did not like being chained in the laundry although he was allowed to run loose in our enclosed yard several times a day. Whenever he was able to get loose from his chain, he would always try to run out into the streets. He would roam to unknown places for several hours, but would always come home. He got loose one day. In his enthusiasm to get out, he scaled the 3-foot high counter in the laundry (as he often did) just as a customer was entering the laundry. The customer got the scare of his life as he saw this 50 pound dog lunging over the counter toward him. He frantically tried to dodge *Beebee Gow*—laughing when he realized that the dog had no interest in him. He only wanted to go out for a romp. *Beebee Gow* is a metaphor for Chinese names, the immigrant spirit, and our inability to change fate. He mirrored our feelings of being trapped by our environment, but always coming home—our bonds and bondage.

Our neighborhood underwent rapid social change with waves of new immigrants displacing the former; the Irish were replaced by the Italians who were then replaced by the Puerto Ricans. We lived on Ellery Street, a street ruled by the local Ellery Bops gang. We would hear of rumbles and avoid getting involved. Sometimes gang members would befriend us and protect us from the taunting intimidation of others. Others would jeer at us chanting racist remarks of: *"Ching Chong"* or *"Chinita, Chinita"* as we made our way to and from the subway five blocks away.

As the rate of burglaries rose, we installed iron gates over the open counter of the laundry and a mirror at the entrance to the laundry to enable my parents to look down the street from the inside. The mirror served another purpose of giving my parents a view to the outside world as they slaved away in the laundry. We would come home from school and do our homework in the apartment above the laundry; my parents were always reminding us about how lucky we were not to have to live in the back of the laundry as so many Chinese immigrant families do.

8 Family with Maternal Godfather, circa 1960

My parents were always working in the laundry downstairs. Sometimes, my sister and I would sneak out to the candy store. The mirror was a dead giveaway so we figured out how to leave the house outside the view of this mirror by clinging to the building wall to avoid detection. I don't know why we did this since my parents were always so busy working, they never noticed; but I was always delighted that I had pulled something over them.

The Dreams of Moving on Up

As the neighborhood changed, so did the hand laundry business. It could no longer financially sustain the family. As children, we were not privy to these matters and did not understand the changes occurring around us. My father tried to start up other businesses in the hope of improving our lot. He was always very mechanical and handy, and enjoyed home fix-it projects. He first tried his hand at construction; however, his perfectionistic tendency made it impossible for him to make a living. He would take too long to complete a project.

He then decided to start up another laundry out in Rockville Center on Long Island. It was his dream to move us out to a better neighborhood if he could make a go of it; that was never to happen. He physically built the laundry from scratch himself and set up shop. He stayed there during the week and only came home on Sundays; he lived in the back of the laundry because he could not afford to rent an apartment. My mother remained alone working the laundry in Brooklyn.

When this laundry venture failed, my father began working in restaurants to bring in extra income. The number of Chinese restaurants grew as Americans began to enjoy chow mein and chop suey dishes—most Americans did not realize that no true Chinese would touch these Western dishes. We considered restaurant work a cut above the work of dealing with dirty laundry and envied our friends whose parents were restaurant owners. Since my father had no restaurant experience, he began as a dishwasher or third chef. As he was not one used to taking orders from others, the stress on him was profound. The handling of food and detergents were harsh on his hands; he developed dermatitis that affected his hands and legs. For many years thereafter, he was unable to work because of the sores oozing from his hands and legs. Despite many visits to doctors, it seemed incurable. My father would bemoan the pain and debilitation he suffered. None of us recognized the psychosomatic aspects of his disorder and the stress had manifested his suffering on his body (See the Ajase Complex in Chapter 1). As a Chinese father and husband, he was too proud; he could not shirk from his family responsibilities or tolerate the humiliation of not being in control of his fate.

With the growing crime rate in the neighborhood, and without my father there "to protect us", we installed an intercom connecting the upstairs apartment and the laundry. The boldness (<u>dai om</u>) of my siblings and mother in foiling several burglary attempts was legendary in our family. One night, a burglar confronted my mother. With characteristic boldness, she ran to the intercom screaming for help. My brother, not heeding any danger, ran down to protect her. The burglar ran off, intimidated by their defiance. Another time, my sister confronted a would-be burglar in the laundry at the cash register upon her return from school. The burglar ran off with my 13 year old sister in hot pursuit. She did justice to her well-earned reputation for her spunkiness.

These harsh circumstances led to dreams of moving from the city. For my parents, the country was symbolic of the China they had left behind. They dreamed of the trees and the flowers, the freedom of open space. This was Islip out on Long Island. Convinced by our neighbors, my parents took a risk and bought a 2 1/4 acre lot in Islip to fulfill their dream. For some years, we would drive three hours each way out there every Sunday. It would be an all-day outing. My father would bring his hatchet to trim the trees. We would pack our food since we could not afford to go to restaurants. There were no facilities of any kind. We would hang out on this piece of land in the woods, and dream of the house that was never to be built. My father would draw detailed floor plans for its construction. He would clear the woods with his hatchet to see if the setting for the house would be just right. This was his dream to own a piece of the Good Earth, to live comfortably in retirement, and to be free. My father died in 1974, never living long enough to see the fulfillment of these dreams.

Forging a Chinese American identity

Attending *Wah Keuh Hok Hau*, a Chinese language school in Manhattan's Chinatown was one of those defining moments that transformed us. As soon as my brother and sister were "old enough", they were enrolled in and attended Chinese School after their regular American School studies. My parents wanted us to learn Chinese and to get a Chinese education. Because they were too busy working in the laundry, they allowed my sister who was merely 8 and my brother who was 9 to travel by subway alone from Brooklyn to Manhattan 5 days a week—a 45 minute ride each way with two changes. At the age of 9, it was my brother's role and responsibility to protect my 8 year old sister. Being the youngest, my mother considered me too young to attend until 4 years later when I was 11.

I begged to go to Chinese School after listening with envy each night to the stories my brother and sister told about the friends they made and the fun they had. I was fascinated hearing about the Ping Pong tournaments, Volleyball games, school picnics, and Drum and Fife Corps in which they participated. I envied the fun my sister had simply throwing spitballs made of toilet paper on the bathroom walls in the school. Chinese school was a place where we all shared a common experience of being Chinese—it was our community, a place in which we were no longer the exotic and strange Chinese.

Most of our peers had a mediocre interest in the scholarship part of Chinese school, which emphasized rote memory drill, and learning the Chinese classics. Many repeated first grade for several years before dropping out. But the social relationships formed and bonding with other Chinese American peers was transforming and reinforced our identities as Chinese Americans.

9 Willie - Drum Corp

We all joined the Chinese School Drum, Bugle, and Fife Corp whether or not we had any musical talent or interest. We did as we were told—marching in parades and celebrating the holidays. We marched in the Chinese Lantern Festival, Lunar New Year and Double Ten Day parades. We marched in the American Thanksgiving parade and successfully competed in contests as a unique Chinese marching band. Yet, our Drum Corps instructor could never get the band past playing our four basic songs: *The Bells of St Mary, Auld Lang Syne, Yankee Doodle, and Battle Hymn of the Republic.* Most of us were not serious musicians having joined the band only for the social bonding. Ironically, I became Fife Sergeant as the remaining senior member.

Few of us were aware of sociopolitical implications of our activities. The Double Ten Festival commemorated the start of the Wuchang Uprising of October 10, 1911 which led to the collapse of the Qing Dynasty and establishment of the Republic of China; we never realized that this demonstrated our community's patriotism to democracy and to the Nationalist Chinese government. We never really understood the fear of deportation experienced by my parents and others in the community if deemed a communist or if discovered to have false identity papers. We dutifully sang the *Star Spangled Banner* at our American school assemblies, and *Sam Ming Ju Yee*, the national anthem of the Republic of China at our Chinese School assemblies. We never questioned the schism between our American and Chinese cultures, and the lack of true freedom felt by our parents.

All we knew was that we were supposed to *Be Chinese and Speak Chinese*, a strong recurring message from our Chinese elders for fear that we would lose our Chinese heritage. The Melting Pot myth of the 1950s, carried the strong recurring message of American patriotism. Yet, we faced daily reminders that Chinese Americans were not truly Americans; we were always asked, "Are you Chinese or Japanese?" by white strangers. At the same time, our Chinese elders would call us *"jook sing"*, a rather derogatory name given to American born Chinese denoting that our brains were like the hollow part of the bamboo—viewed as ignorant of Chinese culture. Ultimately, many of us wore this label with pride in arrogant defiance; we knew who we were.

Being Chinese American was an experience of schisms and contradictions. We spoke Toisanese at home (a village dialect of the peasants), read Cantonese at Chinese school (a city dialect of the urban more refined), and sang the Chinese national anthem in Mandarin (the national dialect of the scholars). We spoke Chinese at home at the insistence of our parents and English at American school at the insistence of our teachers. We were told to be integrated in our identity as one person; yet we were always reminded that we were not true Chinese or American. In our American

10 Anna - Fife Corp

schools, we were asked each year to showcase what the Lunar New Year was all about simply because we were Chinese. I was initially puzzled, and later angry with comments about how good my English skills are—Once a friend's father who was driving me home commented, "I can't tell that you are Chinese by hearing you speak"; I was sitting in the back of the car. Such comments were both patronizing and ignorant. I was expected to speak broken English with an accent although I was born in America?

Family and Community Bonds

As teenagers, we roamed the five short blocks of Chinatown along Mott Street—it was our community. We gave names to the different groups who "hung out" together--"the 37 crowd" lived at 37 Mott Street; the Transfiguration crowd attended the church; the Vikings crowd was members of that volleyball team, and Poy Ching crowd was members of that social club. As our parents made their Sunday outings to the clan associations, we made it out to attend church, meet with friends, and hung out—often taking us several hours to walk the five short blocks of Mott Street as we stopped along the way to chat with friends and make new acquaintances. We often greeted the Chinese elders along the way; and then there were the old Chinese men—the sojourners who lived alone— walking with a slow shuffle and eyes downcast. The *lo faan* tourists came to stare at the exotic sights of Chinese people and roasted meats in the store windows; at night, they were awed by the neon lights of Chinatown.

The Family Clan Association—Dreams and Bondage

As a child, we took the subway every Sunday to go out to New York's Chinatown to hang out at Cher-Long-Fong, (Lau clan association). This was the life behind the neon signs; this was community, family, and culture. The *gong-si-fong* (clan association) members were mostly bachelor husbands or sojourners—laundrymen with wives still in China, ever hopeful to return to China as wealthy men. After China became communist in 1949, little communication with their wives was possible. Most of the men were more concerned with their families than with the politics. They spent their Sundays getting their groceries and then hanging out in the *gong-si-fong* talking and playing cards. One group always played 13-card poker while others engaged in conversation.

The conversations at the *gong-si-fong* often drifted to reminiscing about the good old days in China and their dreams of returning to an idyllic China where the lychees and fruits were sweeter and fresher, the flowers more beautiful, and the scenery far surpassing to be seen in America—it was the dream of paradise—of the Peach Orchard in the Jade Mountain of their minds. The elders endlessly bemoaned their plight in America of struggle and poverty, but would be thankful for having escaped the poverty in China with starvation and illness. At least, there was food to eat here in America.

We were educated from listening to these conversations about one's *tiel meng* (life and fate), and how people were destined to be *ji-woon* (unlucky) or *herng-fook* (prosperous). Not much could be done about fate as they all struggled to make ends meet. Their anguish were felt as they dreamed to retire in comfort back in China with the respect from their home villages. My father shared this dream as he and others tried to make the hardships of working in a laundry more bearable. The elders would commiserate together believing there was no escape from their fate and the bondage they felt.

We heard about the health problems as the elders shared their stories— having gallstones the size of rocks, or sugar in the urine. We heard about the concubines—Uncle so-and-so was a judge in China so he could afford to have so many wives; now Second Wife is angry because Uncle so-and-so is bringing First Wife over. We often pretended to play or sat obediently as we listened with awe.

We often did not understand the psyche of the Chinese elders. We heard their disdain for the *bak guey* (white devils), their mistrust of *lo faan* (Mr. Foreigner or whites), their poker face demeanor or obsequiousness when dealing with whites as a means of protection, their stark boldness disguised to avoid detection, and their energized comradery to give them strength when amidst the privacy of the *gung si fong* (clan association). At times, they expressed outrage at the infamous signs at foreigner hotels in Shanghai, China following World War II—*Chinese and dogs not allowed".* They reiterated these stories as examples of the racist American attitudes and discriminatory behavior toward Chinese people.

The stories were colorful, but spoke of a wall, or perhaps a brocade curtain, that separated them from mainstream America and through which they could not escape. They were bound by the oppression of racism, their psychological isolation, and the burden of poverty as they etched out their lives in America.

Whenever my father was asked about his line of work, his response was always the same, "What is there to do? I work a laundry!" Many of the Chinese elderly men would lament with frustration, "the *lo faan* will not let you do anything else." When feeling more cynical and pessimistic, they often chided us with a discouraging tone, "Look in the mirror at your face!"—this meant you can never change or hide the fact that you are Chinese.

These early Toisanese immigrants remember the feudal governments in China (unlike later Hong Kong immigrants who remember British colonialism and government corruption)—all sought safe haven from this oppression. In the privacy of the *gong si fong,* we heard stories from the Chinese elders about brainwashing and execution under the new communist regime; they compared this political oppression with the racism in America. They debated what was needed to bring China out of a feudal era.

The bachelor husbands always talked of sending money back to their families—their continuing obligation to the families they left behind despite living in impoverished conditions themselves. Most lived in the back of their laundries or shared rooms with other bachelor husbands.

Whenever a letter from China would arrive, it would be circulated at the clan association. A communal reading and discussion would ensue among whoever was in the room—this was an opportunity to connect with those in China even if it was not one's own nuclear family. The elders who were literate would read for those who were not. There was shared anger when relatives were overly demanding for money believing life was so good in America. Everyone gave their opinion or advice. Everyone heard about the news of births, marriages, and deaths.

My parents' letters came from *Sel Ming* (my brother) and *Dai Q* (maternal eldest uncle). My parents would attempt to parent and discipline *Sel Ming* from across the ocean through these letters. The letters from *Dai Q* would report his misbehavior and his unwillingness to study while the letters from *Sel Ming* would plead for a speedy reunion. My parents would write back scolding him and insisting that he listened to *Dai Q and Dai Kim*.

The atmosphere of the *gong-si-fong* was vibrant with multiple conversations going on simultaneously in this small space. Decibel levels rose as men dropped in and out each Sunday afternoon. I learned a lot on these afternoons as I sat obediently near my parents. Conversations were never censored; there were no toys nearby. Instead, we vicariously learned the lessons of life as we listened to these adult conversations.

No *guey lo* (white devil) ever came to visit the *gong si fong*; none were invited. Our clan association consisted of 3 small rooms in a railroad style apartment. Everyone congregated in the small 14x10 living room; in the back was a small kitchen and a small bedroom for bachelor men needing inexpensive, transient sleeping quarters. The association assisted in finding jobs, making loans, social networking, and mutual support. They sometimes settled disputes since Chinese immigrants would not trust the justice system of the American courts.

The Emergence of Women— the first women's clan association

My mother was one of the first wives to immigrate to America, hence one of the few women visiting the clan association during the 1940s and 50s.. I never noticed that my mother was the only woman in the room, and that the men who talked to us had crossed the gender divide. There were the gambling elders playing 13-card poker—the favorite card game of Toisanese men. They played energetically in the corner of the room while carrying on exclusive conversations. They smoked heavily and swore intensely whenever they won or lost a hand. For the most part, they ignored us. Every once in a while, one would win a big hand and give us children a dollar or two to extend his luck. Some of the men talked around us—believing that children and women did not properly belong in their circle of interaction and were not to be heard.

That's why I remembered those who talked to us. There was *Mon Hong Bak* (Uncle Mon Hong), a nice, gentle uncle who was always smiling and might give us a nickel for candy which we would eagerly anticipate. There was his younger brother who we nicknamed *Gee Bak Gai* (Pigsy from

Journey to the West) since he was fat with a huge stomach, and always seemed to be asleep as he sat and listened to the conversation.

This was home base for my parents on a Sunday afternoon in Chinatown for many years. They would do their weekly grocery shopping for Chinese goods not available in our neighborhood markets in Brooklyn and would return to the *gong-si-fong* to socialize before heading home.

Then in the late 1950s, my mother began to visit the *Foo Nul Fong*. I never understood why my father remained at *Cher Long Fong* and would urge her to go by herself. I now realize that this was one of the first women's association in Chinatown—an alternative to the men's *gong si fong*. It was formed by and for immigrant women back as more women immigrated to join their husbands. The atmosphere here was different as women bought their weekly groceries and went there to socialize before going home. However, they always prepared a communal meal each Sunday. My mother enjoyed her visits to this room filled with women and children. .

Our Two Family Clans—Switching Identities

The family clan or extended family is the backbone of Chinese culture. Honorific titles are used for all familial relationships to designate their status—their order in the family hierarchy and the paternal or maternal lineage. Honorific titles of uncle or aunt are created for friends as a way of including them into the extended family—(*Ah Suk and Ah Bahk* for Younger and Elder Paternal Uncle or *Ah Seem and Ah Mo* for Younger and Elder Paternal Aunt). Neighbors from the same village in China are designated as *Hong Ah Suk or Hong Ah Bahk* meaning uncles from the same village.

Whereas we had few first order relatives in America, my father would honor more distant relatives because they were our closest relatives here in America. Whenever we met anyone new, my parents always discussed with them the status of the relationship between my father and the other man to decide which honorific title would be used in addressing one another.

Because my mother considered herself fortunate to be one of the early wives to join her husband here in America among the many bachelor husbands, she took it upon herself to watch over the other bachelor husbands in the clan. During the Chinese holidays, she would make extra pastries to give to them. We would deliver these pastries during the Lunar New Year, and looked forward to the *hung bow* (red envelopes with money) we would receive in return. We were taught to make an initial protest that it was unnecessary (*mm-soy*) so as not to appear greedy; but we always knew they would insight on our accepting the *hung bow*, and we would be complimented for our good manners. We were taught to always properly thank them using their honorific title. We could see the delight in the elders whenever we came with these gifts. They saw in us what we did not—the future and their hope. We spoke English; we could negotiate the mainstream environment in ways they felt they never would.

While *Cher-Long-Fong* was the clan association where my parents connected and gained support during the 1940s-50s. As mentioned earlier, my father was born a Lau, adopted as a Lee, and immigrated to America under identity papers as a Lau. Initially, we had no Lee relatives here in America. As our Lee relatives began to immigrate here, my father felt torn between his dual loyalties. He feared the Lau clan, who befriended him and helped him get started, would disapprove and reject him for being disloyal if he associated with the Lees. On the other hand, he feared the Lee clan would accuse him of being ungrateful to his adopted family by returning to the Lau clan. To resolve this dilemma, we maintained dual identities and social ties with both clans. However, we were coached never to mention that we were a Lau in front of our Lee relatives and vice versa. As children, we walked around with this secret, never really understanding why it was all so important; we knew we had to switch identities (Lee or Lau) depending on whom we were with.

As an adult, I visited some maternal relatives in Canada with my maternal uncle, <u>Poy Q</u>. When asked my surname, I stammered forgetting which one to use and said Lau. My uncle gently corrected me saying we were Lee attributing my confusion and ignorance to being *jook sing* (American born Chinese).

We were always switching identities. In addition to our two clans, we also had paper relatives who we sometimes visited. We treated them with more distance since there was no "real" family relationship. Always in fear of being deported, my parents insisted on our American names being Lau, but enrolled us in Chinese School as Lees, our "real" identities. We were coached never tell this to the *lo faan* because it would jeopardize our immigration status. We carefully memorized our paper identities and avoided probing questions by white people about our identities.

This all changed after the Family Reunification Act of 1965. For years, we were trained to hide our true identities; now we needed to come clean and confess if we had any hope of bringing our families over from China. My father "confessed" his true identity as did so many other Chinese immigrants. He legally changed his name to Kim Lau Lee to honor his adopted parents, but retained his ties to his biological parents. This act threw all of us children into a new identity crisis as we tried to integrate parts of our identities that we had kept separate all our lives. This act made it possible for my mother to begin proceedings to bring over *Sel Ming*, the son she had left in China over 25 years ago, though this was not to happen for another 25 years.

Our Chinese American Culture—Character Training

11 My mother's 60th birthday

My mother enjoyed good music and good story. The classical Chinese stories discussed in Chapter 1 were part of our moral training as it was for most Chinese immigrant children. I recall hearing the story of *The Three Moves of Mencius* many times which celebrates a mother's wisdom, the value placed on scholarship, and the importance of environment on a child's upbringing—intended for our character training.

For a time, my mother took us to the Chinese movies on a weekly basis. The martial arts movies typically featured mystical feats that defy gravity and gung-fu warriors with fantastical speeds and skills. We would laugh in disbelief while my mother would explain the hidden powers of the wind and the strength of one's inner *Qi* (force) in the Chinese culture accomplished only after vigorous training. It was not until the contemporary Bruce Lee and Jackie Chan martial arts movies became popular in the West that we could appreciate this aspect of Chinese culture.

When live Chinese opera came to town, we attended these performances known as *Dai Hay* or big performances. My sister hated the opera with its jarring, falsetto high tones, which she said gave her headaches. Afterwards, my mother would teach me some of the songs in Mandarin. She always took delight in being able to speak Mandarin having lived in Nanjing. Together we would listen to the music and rehearse the lyrics, singing the songs together over and over again. She was delighted and so proud when I could finally sing two of these songs on my own although I never could remember what the words meant.

Chinese opera, martial arts and classic Chinese stories contrasted with our interest in Rock and Roll music of the 1950s and 1960s. Elvis Presley was our hero together with the craze of make-up, crinolines, and teased hair during our adolescence. My sister and I would wear 8 starched crinolines under full circle skirts. Each day, we carefully layered each crinoline over one another to fluff it out so that we stood out like Chinese southern belles. We often dressed up in Chinese *cheong saam* (mandarin collar dress with side slits) to attend the dance parties. These visual contrasts in music, story, and dress illustrated our seamless switches between the Chinese and American cultures.

Chinese theaters were notorious for the theatergoers carrying on conversations and socializing while performances were in progress. While my sister complained of the noise in Chinese operas, my parents complained of the noise in Rock and Roll music. My sister and I would go into the record store to buy a 45 rpm record, and spend hours selecting a hit tune. We resonated with the liveliness, loudness, and rhythm of Rock and Roll music and tried to remain oblivious to the gripping fears of the McCarthy era and a racist society.

In addition to the "classic" Chinese stories my mother used for our moral character training, she also told stories about defining moments in our lives which illustrated our character. As she retold these stories to friends and relatives, her image of our character was defined..

My brother was the "protective one"," as any good brother should be. When he was no more than three or four years old, I had put a hook in my eye. Seeing the danger, he ran over and pulled it out of my eye leaving a scar that I still have. To my parents, my brother quick action saved me. Chinese culture demands much of their first born son. He is the one to carry on the family line and must fulfill the obligation and debt to the family. My brother's adolescence was turbulent as the tension between he and my father escalated over these demands and expectations between a Chinese father and his son.

My sister, on the other hand, was the "spunky one." She would stand up to my father when no one else would. He was a tyrant in the manner of a Chinese father who expected unquestioning obedience and respect. When she was no older than ten, my father lost his temper with her and threatened to hit her. My parents kept a switch over the door which they periodically used for physical discipline; this visual symbol of their authority and threat of physical punishment was more frightening than the reality. My sister retaliated with her own threat "to pluck his eyes out and dip it in white sugar for eating." My father was reportedly so impressed with her audacity that he let his guard down and laughed.

I was remembered for my "generosity" (being *dai len*). One day at *Cher Long Fong*, my brother, sister and I all had ice cream cones. My sister dropped hers and reached to take my brother's cone. As he started to cry, I was said to have gone over and offer my ice cream cone to my sister. All the relatives watching were impressed with how I could be so *dai len* at the age of 5. I, however, remember my "curiosity". When I was five and home alone, I climbed up on the kitchen table and stuck my finger into a live electric socket to see what it would do. I got the shock of my life and was so scared I never dared to tell anyone.

Through the music and stories, we became Chinese Americans. The brocade curtain closing China to the West in 1949 fueled paranoia among white Americans of communism, and fear among Chinese Americans of retaliation and racism in America. It was not until the 1960s that the Civil Rights Movement and Women's movement of the 1960s brought new hope and idealism. I began to pursue my social justice ideals while my mother pursued to fulfill her obligation and promise of 50 years to bring her son to America. Civil Rights leader Martin Luther King and President John F. Kennedy bore the hope for of a socially just nation with dreams of reaching the moon, only to be shattered by their assassinations which cut short our hopes that it was to be an easy journey. It was not until President Richard Nixon's trip to China in 1971 that our worlds were brought together once again. Communist China was now open to the West, and Chinese Americans suddenly could entertain hopes of reuniting with their families in China.

12 My parents and Poy Q -1972

My parents visited China in 1972, more than 30 years after my mother left. Like so many of their fellow immigrants, they visited in search of the China they had left behind. The pictures of my parents in Mao Tze Tung jackets were an anomaly we could not reconcile. What my parents found was a China so different that they realized that the idyllic China they sought was with them all along—in their hearts and in the Chinatown community that they had created in America

CHAPTER 6: OUR JOURNEYS— CONNECTING WITH THE PAST

Though her immigration from Toisan spanned 8,000 miles across the ocean, my mother dared not venture beyond the confines of her Chinatown community unaccompanied during her 55 years in America. When living in Brooklyn, she primarily went to Manhattan's Chinatown. After I married and moved to Boston, our vacations brought her to places far away. We visited places as far as magnificent as the Great Wall of China, as reminiscent as her hometown of Nanjing China, as foreign as the streets of Paris, and as awesome as the volcano eruptions on the big island of Hawaii. We traveled north to Ottawa, Canada where her half-sister had immigrated, south to Florida's Disney World, west to the Golden Mountains of California where the Lau clan now resided, and east to China. As we visited the four corners of the earth, my mother would exclaim, "In my days as a laundrywoman, these are places I never even dreamed about."

Our Vacations--Intergenerational Bonds

And so, my mother and I journeyed together. Our vacations became an avenue for us to remain connected. As my mother joined my husband and two children for our annual vacations, the generations bonded. I got to see my mother while she became the mother to my husband and the grandmother to my children—an opportunity we never had as children.

Her stories, as recounted in Part II of this book, filled our time as her voice connected with the voices from past; and we bonded through the images in the present. I heard the wisdom of her simple words. I heard the anguish of her experience. I heard the bondage of her life As we traveled, I saw the world through her eyes and mine. I saw in her the pioneering spirit, but the villager at heart. I felt her plight of lifelong longing and guilt for those she left behind. I felt her never ending hope for us, her children, not to have to suffer as she did. The paradoxes between us were many. I had my doctorate while my mother had only a sixth grade education. We were both well-traveled; but she remained confined to Chinatown while my horizons had expanded. We grew up in two different worlds—she after the turn of the 20th century in the first year of the Republic of China, me a post-World War II baby. Yet, it was she who mentored me.

13 My mother and grandchildren, circa 1970

The 1970s and 1980s were transformational, not only in our vacations together, but also because this was the era of the Vietnam War, Flower Children, Peace Movement, and Me Generation. As a society, we sought peace in the 1990s, but for me, it was the end of an era met with trauma. My mother died in 1994; hit by a car as she crossed the street to go home to Confucius Plaza in the supposedly protected confines of Chinatown. Following her death, these renewed ties abruptly ended, as I would no longer travel that journey with her again. I struggled with how to make sense of the senseless just as we as a nation struggled with the senseless assassinations and terrorism. So traumatized were we by my mother's death that my siblings and I could barely cross the street without fear and pain, knowing that her life ended in such tragedy.

Seventy-Two Adventures—Completing the Journey

Monkey King is capable of 72 possible transformations—symbolic of the adventures in our journeys. My 72 year old mother, husband, 3 year old son and I visited China in 1981 while I was pregnant. My mother had yearned for a return trip to China after my father died in 1974. Their trip in 1972 had been curtailed because of his health.

My father's trip back to China at the age of 72 after leaving almost 40 years ago was a disappointment he never openly admitted. He found he no longer belonged. His dream of returning to an idyllic China that kept him going and enabled him to struggle with the poverty, racism, and hardships of making a living was shattered. China and he had changed; he realized that he could no longer live there; he died 2 years later of emphysema.

My mother looked to me to complete the journey that was never finished with my father. For my mother, our trip was a dream come true. While she was from China, she had never "seen" China. As a child, she was told of the wonders of China, but she never dreamed that she would see the magnificence of the Great Wall, the natural beauty of Guilin, the industrialized Shanghai, the celebrated beauty of the women in Hangzhou, or the opulence of the Summer Palace. We were both in awe as we approached the Summer Palace; here were a 74 year old grandmother and a pregnant mother in sweltering 90-degree heat together trying to climb the 1,000 steps of their journey to the top.

I was amazed at Shanghai's industrialization and the Western influence in the architecture, while my mother remembered how the Western powers had been so cunning and deceptive in reaching an agreement with China to divide up Shanghai during World War II. According to my mother, the Western powers told China that they just wanted to occupy land the size of a water buffalo. China acquiesced only to find that the Western powers had cut up the sinews of the water buffalo into one long string, and stretched it into one large circle, thereby surrounding all of Shanghai. To add insult to injury, they then prohibited the Chinese from using the public gardens, with posted signs that said, "No dogs or Chinese allowed". As her self-esteem and national pride swelled up, I could feel the shame and injury in my mother's tone of voice.

The trip to China was an opportunity for reunions as much as it was for seeing the sights. In Nanjing, my mother reunited with *Sel Ming*, her son whom she had seen only once in 1972 after she left him in 1939, 42 years before. I met my older brother for the first time when he was 47. He was married with 4 grown children. Although we were brother and sister, our lives could not have been more different. Our communication difficulties could not be more symbolic, as his children and I spoke different dialects. They knew little about my life in the United States, and could not fathom the amenities to which we were accustomed. Though Sel Ming now lived a middle class life, his family had no running water in the house; toilet facilities were a block away in an outhouse; and their one sink for a family of 6 was outside the front door. One loft served as the sleeping quarters for the entire family while the floors were natural dirt floors. Suddenly, I understood the books I used to read at Chinese school describing the need to spray down a floor to clean it and keep the dust down.

After spending a week with Sel Ming, the pain my mother felt in having to leave him once again was rekindled in my memory. I could feel her anguish, and imagine the resurgence of that moment when he woke up to find her gone. This moment resurrected all the abandonment guilt she felt, and her helpless inability to change her fate.

Almost 25 people came to the airport, waiting all day to meet us (because I had not wanted to inconvenience them by telling them my flight arrival time). There was a different sense of time. Parading before me now were all the relatives in the stories from my mother's past including Ah Yee, my mother's half-sister, and her husband Yee Cherng (husband of Younger Maternal Aunt), and the children of *Dai Q,* my mother's brother. All of Dai Q's children had become doctors or pharmacists, and were well educated. My *Yee Cherng,* was an accountant. I saw my mother stuck in a time warp; she was the one who had the courage to venture overseas.

14 My mother and grandchildren in Nanjing-1981

We had all heard stories of one another through the letters my mother had written over the years. Now the stories we exchanged about our lives gave a new sense of reality; my mother's life in the laundry was not one of luxury or comfort. Although she, with her sixth grade education, have been the one to provide them with financial support, their educational achievements matched mine.

As we toured Nanjing, my mother sought out the building that had once been owned by my grandfather, *Ah Gung.* My mother had heard that property in China could be reclaimed by overseas Chinese; as we searched, my relatives quietly tell me that under communism, the government had taken over all properties. My mother remembered anew the atrocities of the Japanese during the Rape of Nanking. It was clear that she was still traumatized by her escape after more than 40 years.

My mother also learned how much she had changed. Although we viewed my mother as so Chinese, my *Yee Cherng* said it was clear she was from the United States. When I asked how people could tell, he said with affection, "Look at the way she dresses. It is risqué showing her shoulders at her age. And all that color." My mother was wearing a sleeveless, conservative (or so I thought) gray and black print dress. I then realized that women over 50 in China wore nothing but plain black or brown, and covered their shoulders even in very hot weather.

One Hundred Years of Good Fortune

One hundred is the number Chinese give when they want to give you a blessing. It is comparable to infinity. So it is common to wish *"May you live a 100 years!"* When we left Nanjing, *Ah Yee* gave my mother a beautiful, satin brocade cloth embroidered with 100 children. It was her wish for my mother to be blessed with a 100 offspring (usually including grandchildren and great-grandchildren).

In Beijing, we met with the eldest son of my *Dai Q* (eldest maternal uncle), *Fei Gong*. For my mother, it was to be her last reunion; she treated the visit as a reconnection with family whom she had never expected to see again. Her special bond to *Fei Gong* as the eldest son of her elder brother and primary link in the ancestral line to her father was evident. In return, *Fei Gong* treated her and us with the utmost of respect; she was his *Dai Goo* (eldest of the younger paternal aunt) of his father who had already passed away. He escorted us to the Great Wall of China and the Heavenly Temple of Beijing. Fei Gong's behavior was consistent with Confucian principles of ancient China, where the emperor was regarded as the "Son of Heaven", who administered matters on the earth on behalf of the heavenly authority.

Volcanic Eruptions

15 My mother - Hawaii volcano

We visited the big island in Hawaii while the volcano of Hilo was active and erupting; lava was flowing from the mountaintop to the sea. Since I did not have the Chinese vocabulary to inform my mother where we were going; I could not tell her what we were about to see. The sight of the erupting volcano was beyond her wildest imagination. At first, she wondered what the fiery, soft, molten, gray lava was. When I pointed from where it was flowing, there was disbelief at first. She said, "These are wonders about which you hear; never ones that I thought I would see." .My own awe in seeing this once in a lifetime event was enhanced--sandwiched between the awe of my mother and that of my children. My mother reacted like a child—the grandmother more enthralled than my children at this natural wonder. She rushed to examine the lava, and to collect what she could as a memoir to bring home.

Ancestry Revisited

We traveled to many cities within the United States. As we reached each destination, my mother always had a name and address of someone from her past. that she would ask me to look up. These were people whom I heard about growing up, people my mother never would have reconnected with had we not been traveling together. Suddenly, there were faces to the stories my mother told—like ghosts from the past. Suddenly, her experiences were made more real as I heard their affirmation from others

In the years to follow, we reunited with Wong friends and relatives in Vancouver, Toronto, Seattle, Los Angeles, San Francisco, Ottawa, and Texas—relatives, childhood friends, and village sisters (*hong ah jeer*) from Hoiping village. One *hong ah jeer*, in her 80s, was shocked and delighted to see my mother; she reminisced with my mother and shared stories of the village, of their youth, and how they were so close they even shared a bed together. As I watched the glow in my mother's face, I connected with the past and revisited my ancestry. Our history was now in the present. As I watched my mother's face beam with joy, and listened to her voice filled with excitement, I thought to myself, "These are experiences I would only have dreamed of."

On our visit to Los Angeles in 1992, I was in for the surprise of my life. We had looked up a relative with *Ah Koon Seem,* my paternal aunt from the Lau clan. The visit was quite enjoyable as my mother once again exchanged stories of life in China. Because of my mother's poor hearing, *Ah Koon Seem* told me (rather than my mother) that she wanted to bring us to visit some relatives. Not able to keep names and honorific titles of extended family relatives from the Lau and Lee clans straight, and hampered by my need to translate Chinese names into their English equivalent, I acquiesced. I did not fully realize the significance of the people we were to meet until we sat around the table in the restaurant. I realized that we were talking to my father's nephew, *Sam Suk*'s son (paternal younger uncle number 3), and my father's half-sister, *Ah Dai Goo* from the Lau clan, the biological family who abandoned him as an infant. In my youth, these relatives would write to my father with hardship stories asking for money. Always angered by these letters because my father believed the stories were embellished, my father nevertheless always sent them some money. Neither my siblings nor I ever knew that they had made it to the United States, and were living in Los Angeles. *Sam Suk* was infamous for his cunning and his exploitation of others for money. Because of my father's loyalty to his birth parents, he gave in to these appeals for money.

For the first time, I watched my mother freeze in her social interaction. Typically energetic and overjoyed at meeting with people from her past, and always ready to share stories and memories, I saw my mother become silent and angry. I was bewildered and could not understand. After we left, my mother expressed her anger. She reminded me of how her *Lau Lo Yeer* (Lau father-in-law) had accused her of being restless and not watchful of the home as she waited for my father in China; this implied that she was not virtuous. My mother emphatically said she had no interest in meeting them. Only then did I realize how much this had been an assault to her character and integrity. As generous and forgiving as my mother was, this was unforgivable.

16 My mother, Scott, Stephen - 1993 Ottawa

We traveled to Ottawa, Canada in 1993, and reunited for the last time with my mother's half-sister, *Ah Yee*. My mother and Ah Yee were able to transcend the past, reconnect in the present, and bond as sisters with the Wong relatives on my mother's side. This seem to make up for the many years where my mother bemoaned the fact that she did not have relatives nearby.. On this visit. we had reunited four generations of children, grandchildren, and great-grandchildren with my mother and Ah Yee.

When we did not travel, my mother would visit me in Massachusetts. She would never stay long for fear of intruding. She refused to live with any one of her children despite our urging contrary to Chinese tradition. She constantly reminded me of my father's words "Don't live with the children if you want to remain independent!" Always nurturing and supportive, she would mend our clothes, hem my husband's pants, cook up special dishes, clean or organize my kitchen cabinets while I was away at work. She never complained always acknowledging our busy work schedules. I was always grateful for her visits, but torn between juggling my work and keeping her entertained. My mother often brought "care packages" for us—Chinese dry foods and herbal tonic ingredients that she did not think I knew about or had the time to buy. She would label each package and write down the instructions for using the ingredients in Chinese. It was as if she intended to ensure that this knowledge would be passed on to posterity.

Reunion after 50 years

Through the years, my mother always remembered *Sel Ming*—her son. She reminded us each year to send him money for the Lunar New Year. It was she who wrote to him to keep in touch. She never gave up her motherly guidance and never forgot her obligation and promise. It was she who wrote to chastise him for some reported misdeed, or to criticize him for his grammatical mistakes, insisting that he improve his writing skills. After my father's death, she renewed her vigor in fulfilling that promise with my brother's help. Since Sel Ming had been adopted, my mother had to legally prove that he was my father's son. He reliance on dates were committed to memory rather than paper,. and was sometimes contradictory. Through her perseverance, she finally reunited with him 50 years later when he came to live in the United States at age 55.

17 Reunion after 50 years

By then, he was a grandfather. *Sel Ming* arrived with his wife to rejoin my mother. Both could now complete their journey; my mother had completed her obligation. She had absolved her guilt. Having provided financial support to him all his life, she now felt it was his turn to show the filial piety due to her as his mother. It was her expectation that he become all that she expected of her eldest son.

For *Sel Ming*, the 50 years of separation, of yearning to be with his mother, of coming to America to join his family were now over. We can only guess what his dreams might have been about his missed opportunities that we, his siblings, enjoyed in the United States. But the pain and anguish of mother-son separation over the course 50 years do not

disappear with a reunion. As reality set in, it became clear that the reunion could not heal these wounds. *Sel Ming* and his wife lived with my mother to get himself settled, but the mother-son relationship that had been absent during the 50 years of separation was simulated.

As they renegotiated their mother-son relationship now as great-grandmother and grandfather, the anguish remained. My mother expected him to be grateful for the years she spent in anguish to keep her promise to him. She had supported him for years long after she had stopped supporting her children in the U.S. She had suffered much hardship fighting with my father to keep her promise. *Sel Ming*, on the other hand, expected her to make up for the years he had lost, for the years he had waited, for his years without a mother. He observed the huge material contrasts between himself and us, and could not help but think what his life would have been like if she had not left him. Now that mother and son were reunited, they could finally be angry at each other. My mother could never understand *Sel Ming's* anguish; she believed it was a son's obligation to honor his parents. My father never lived to see this reunion.

PART III: TRANSFORMATION AND ENLIGHTENMENT

18 My Mother's 70th Birthday

Two images stand out in the Journey to the West made by Chinese immigrant families. The Chinese woman warrior fought the battles against loss, poverty, trauma, and racism. Their journey of immigration posed many challenges and trials for them to face and resolve. As warriors on a sojourn to renew their identity, they were transformed and enlightened as they achieved a positive bicultural identity,

For Chinese immigrants, this may mean not an integrated identity, but rather one of multiple or bicultural identities, much like an egg where the yolk is separate from the albumin—the yin and the yang which are complementary. The developmental task is not acculturation to a Western way of life, but biculturalism toward a new identity that is enriching amidst the contradictions and paradoxes of both Asian and Western ways.

Sometimes the cultural myths and stories get lost as second and third generation immigrant families travel through the ages; they lose their culture and their identities. The next generation often seeks to reconnect with their roots and ancestry as they make their journey.

As Monkey King journeyed to the Jade Mountain of the West in search of enlightenment, our Western sisters and brothers journeyed to the Garden of Eden in the East in search of knowledge. Early American pioneers who were Westward bound, while Chinese American pioneers were Eastward bound in search of the Golden Mountains of the west—

they met in California.

191 Mother-Daughter-Grandchildren Scott and Stephen

Part III ends with integrating mythology and storytelling into the immigration story. While the intergenerational saga in this book is about one family who is uniquely Chinese American, all immigrant families must grapple the never ending themes of bonds and bondage. The lessons in Chapter 8 are intended advise readers about what they must do to heal, to grow and to bond. All immigrant families must leave a legacy for their children and grandchildren—they must create their family legend.

CHAPTER 7: OF BONDS AND BONDAGE

Women's connectedness often provides the bonds for immigrant families to preserve and tell their stories. It is in these stories that intergenerational bonds are created. At the same time, the psychological bondage often hovers over preventing escape from the confines of our minds or the boundaries of our cultures. As the journey continues, each family must draw on its own stories and cultural histories to create its own family legend.

Cultural symbols and myths, beliefs and values can both help immigrant families form bonds as well as put them in bondage. While values and beliefs are the basis for the connectedness that bring them together, these same values and beliefs can force immigrant families to narrow their experiences and restrict their boundaries of assimilation. Chinese immigrant families can remain sheltered in ethnic Chinatowns without ever speaking English or communicating with white Americans. Differing perspectives of the same sociopolitical contexts about China or the United States can further distance immigrant families from the mainstream.

The bonds and bondage of these cultural symbols, myths, beliefs and values infuse themselves into the day-by-day living of all immigrant families. To achieve enlightenment, immigrant families must make the journey and create their own family legend to sustain their bicultural identities and to bond them through the generations.

Chinese American Identity

What is a Chinese American? I always knew I was Chinese for as long as I could remember. My parents and all who met me ingrained it in me. The first question I was always asked growing up was: "Are you Chinese or Japanese?" I would always answer "Chinese" before we could go on. Not until I traveled to Europe as an adult did I come to the jolting realization that I was also American. This was the era of the "Ugly American", known for their vulgarity in dress and manners, uninitiated into the more refined customs of European culture, and accustomed to the excesses of material spending with newfound wealth. While going through customs on a highway in Germany, the customs officer, never having seen an Asian face before, asked me the usual question with a smile: "Chinois?" (Chinese?) to which I promptly replied, "Yes" as I always have. Much to my surprise, he was outraged, upon looking at my passport, that I would be so audacious as to try to pass myself off as Chinese when "You're an American!"

Sociopolitical Contexts

Racism and the sociopolitical context were realities that coerced us to ponder the meaning of "Who am I?" as we grew up in America. The melting pot myth said we would all blend together. Yet, the daily questioning prevented us from blending into the great American melting pot. The melting pot was a symbol created to give meaning to and instill patriotism in European white immigrants; it had little meaning for most Chinese immigrants because their inability to blend excluded them from partaking as full citizens in American society. As Americans began to realize the "melting pot" myth, the "salad bowl" became the symbol to address the diversity of racial and cultural differences among Americans—now being important to value and savor the distinct cultures and their unique characteristics.

The Yellow Peril symbol of the McCarthy era of the 1940s and 1950s made Chinese the enemies of democracy given the rise of communism in China, and the economic threat to jobs—fueling an era of fear and paranoia. My parents' only means of getting news was through the Chinese media. They were so fearful of being called a communist and un-American by distrustful white Americans that they burned their Chinese newspapers rather than putting them in the trash to avoid their being mistaken for Communist propaganda. We became secretive for fear of being deported. The Civil Rights and Women's movements of the 60s and 70s were symbols of social change and equity for all. This ideological shift from cultural paranoia to valuing differences gave us renewed hope for peace and a new society with President John F. Kennedy's promise to take us to the moon.—This was the era of Camelot, the myth created by Theodore H. White as he memorialized JFK's death with the words, "Don't let it be forgot, that once there was a spot, for one brief shining moment that was known as Camelot."

As we grew up in America, our experiences mirrored the sociopolitical context of which we were a part. My family had many dinner table conversations when my father, after his evening dinner drink of scotch, would begin his tirade about the ineptness of the current American government. While his criticism was intense, he never felt he had the power to change it. As children, we would become impatient and tell him, "Go back to China". We were more optimistic as we believed we could change everything—Were we not the promise of our parents' pilgrimage to the West?

By 1965, the Family Reunification enabled Chinese American immigrants, long separated from their families in China, to be reunited. Husbands reunited with their wives, fathers with their children. We learned that we had established a new culture that was uniquely Chinese American though my parents and society had insisted that we were Chinese. We began to realize that East and West sometimes cannot meet, but must be complementary as in the yin-yang balances of biculturalism.

Year of the Monkey

I was born the year of the monkey. Early Toisanese Chinese immigrants were known for their adventurous and rebellious spirit, not unlike Monkey King who was loved for his cunning, intelligence, boldness and defiance. His rebelliousness stands in good stead as immigrants faced the racism and struggles of the melting pot myth. In trying to make a living, to survive, they too faced the 81 trials of Monkey King to discern truth from falsehood, demons from the good spirits. My parents' trials included their inability to speak English and the absence of economic opportunities in this land of freedom.

Cultural Bonds and Bondage

In most patriarchal cultures, it is the women who sustain the cultural bonds while the men create the family contexts. As Chinese immigrant families strived to recreate the home, family, and community that they had left behind, they created the Chinatowns as safe havens to retain the culture. The Chinese hand laundries that became the primary means for jobs and survival among the Toisanese also limited and put them in bondage. When they could not step outside the prescribed roles and perceptions, Chinese immigrant families could not create their own self-definitions and colluded with the white mainstream society to make them exotic and foreign.

As immigrant families made their journey, they bonded across the generations. Yet, these very bonds also put them in bondage, linking them inexplicably to an inescapable fate. As Chinese immigrants left their families, their culture and their country behind, their abandonment guilt was often lifelong. I watched as my mother struggled with this guilt that led to her never ending anguish.

The irony is that cultural myths and symbols have helped immigrant families to create common bonds while also keeping in lifelong bondage. The journey of immigration often creates feelings of helplessness and hopelessness as immigrant families face the oppression of racism, the clash of cultures and the subordination of women.

The bondage of culture is not unlike foot binding, a practice begun in the Sung dynasty (960-976 BC), reportedly to imitate an imperial concubine who was required to dance with her feet bound. By the 12th century, the practice was widespread until the establishment of the Republic of China in 1911. Chinese women with small feet were considered beautiful; therefore, girls had their feet bound to maintain their small size. With the constriction of natural growth, the feet became deformed and women were unable to walk. Bound feet symbolize the bondage imposed upon women in distorted values about feminine beauty. These practices became defunct as women's roles as laborers in an agrarian society overtook that of women courtesans in a feudal society. This is a lesson from our past so that immigrants do not continue this bondage.

Poverty amidst Plenty

America was the land of plenty, or so we were told. We read the schoolbooks that mirrored what we thought was the lives of white Americans. Only the Dick and Jane characters in white suburbia where everyone lived in a "white house with a picket fence" and each child had his or her own bedroom did not look like our home.

Despite our poverty, my mother created a home and a culture for us in Brooklyn during a time where few Chinese women could immigrate to America. Despite the labor laws restricting the Chinese to menial jobs, and anti-Chinese legislation restricting immigration,. the early Chinese immigrants were criticized for creating bachelor societies, and living in squalid conditions. However, many Chinese accepted these conditions as, at least, better than those back in China.

As the economy became depressed, and our laundry business declined, there was not enough to make ends meet, my mother began "bootlegging" to supplement our income because my parents were too proud to ask for handouts. She would brew rice wine at home once a month, and bottled it into gallon jugs to be sold to relatives and friends. Since we had no car, we would deliver these gallon jugs by subway, carrying them two at a time. We were urged to be very secretive about this for fear that we would be arrested. But I remember how my mother would beam with pride when an eager customer complimented her; her humility did not allow her to brag, but her face waited in anticipation of the compliment.

When it wasn't there, money was ever so important as a measure of prosperity. Thus, the Toisanese Chinese feel no qualms about asking you how much you make, or how much something costs. Steeped in poverty and the agrarian culture from which they came, they barely had a window to the lives of the rich. So when my father visited me in my new home in the suburbs of Worcester, Massachusetts, he kept mumbling as he wandered through the house, "rich man's house". Yet, he could not tell me the pride he felt about our accomplishment, or of his discomfort of being out of place in his daughter's home. Having lived a life of struggle and poverty, he could not reconcile himself to the comforts of middle class living. He remained poor in his mind; his identity was that of a proud, but poor man. He was proud of his Chinese identity, as a man of integrity, and one who fought for what was right even if it meant physical risk.

Survival in America

We lived in a small 4-room railroad apartment, and were often told how lucky we were that we were not living in the back of the laundry. My brother, sister, and I shared the largest room intended as the parlor while my parents took the 9x9 bedroom. There remained the kitchen with the bathtub until my father built an enclosed bathroom, and a 9x9 living room. Our bedroom had one chest of drawers for the entire family with each of us allocated to one drawer. Mine was the smallest since I was the youngest. We all shared one small closet so we stacked our possessions at the foot of

20 Family - Ellery Street Apartment circa 1950s

the beds. We were so excited when my parents finally got their own chest of drawers.

While we kept a clean apartment, that did not stop the roaches. Living in an old neighborhood in Brooklyn, our repeated spraying and fumigation were to no avail; the roaches survived as did we in these dismal circumstances. When we entered the apartment at night, we would have to walk halfway into a dark room to open the light switch located in the middle of the room. (Note my automatic

Chinese translation of turning on the light which I did not realize until my son Scott called it to my attention.) We were always ready for those roaches before we opened the light; the roaches would scatter as we began to stomp on hundreds of roaches. This was poverty--only we didn't call it that.

There was no privacy in these railroad apartments where you could see straight through the apartment from the kitchen. We closed off one of the two entrances to create more room and entered through the kitchen. Our bedroom had the only window looking out to the street so my father often entered our room to peer out the window. As teenagers, we began to change behind the closet door or in the bathroom to get privacy. When my brother went away to college, my sister conspired with me to create our own bedroom. We moved all his belongings into the living room, and left him the open up couch as his bed.

We rarely ate out at restaurants because it was considered too expensive. On those rare occasions, my father would order one order of GuangDong Chow Mein for the entire family. We could never buy things we wanted because they were always too expensive. We never could afford the clothes our white American peers wore, and always counted the money or asked the price before we bought anything. As we struggled, we wondered if this was indeed the land of freedom and opportunity.

Remembering the Poverty in China

As children, we could never understand why my parents emphasized some things all the time. "You must serve a chicken to celebrate someone's birthday." "Don't show your true feelings because they will take advantage of you." "You must study and work hard." These admonitions were constant and repetitive. Sometimes we became irritated. Other times, we simply ignored them. We were always reminded to finish our rice because of all the people starving in China as well as the beggars in the streets. We would impatiently and jokingly tell my mother to send it back to them. My mother often told pitiful stories of women who were so poor that they could not produce breast milk to nurse their starving children or of how a family of four had to share one bowl of rice for dinner.

Poverty in China often created painful experiences; parents often played favorites or neglected the needs of children in their charge given the limited resources with not enough to go around. Its impact on the psyche was significant in that Toisanese immigrants often continued to hoard or remain thrifty long after their economic conditions have improved. Many were compelled to always demonstrate that they were not impoverished. For example, immigrant families may insist on having their own holiday meal even though they had accepted an invitation to another celebration for fear of being pitied or bear the shame of watching others eat--a bondage that persisted.

The stories of poverty told by my mother never generated the sympathy from us that she wanted. As Chinese Americans, we were arrogant; we could not know poverty and starvation because we never went without a meal. Only as an adult could I realize how my parents' experiences of poverty and starvation back in China shaped their world views forever— how they felt compelled to make these admonitions in the continuing fear that they might experience such hardships once again.

Forever influenced by her past experiences of starvation and as a good Chinese mother, my mother would save the best pieces of food for us while she ate the least desired during any meal we would have together. This was a mother's love; in this way, she could show how much she cared and sacrificed for us. My mother was always generous with others, and frugal with herself. She believed this was one of the highest virtues she could achieve as a woman.

Even as our economic circumstances improved during my adulthood, my mother could never give up her thrifty mentality. My mother and I often shopped together as one of our past times together. She and I loved to hunt for bargains, but she never felt comfortable in the expensive department stores. When shopping together, she would look at the price tags, and cringe in shock and horror; she would always widen her eyes in amazement at the high cost of things. She would wear rags and mend things well beyond their useful life (by our standards). Though she was appreciative of our gifts to honor her, she kept many of them unused for years; ultimately, she would give them away because they were too good for her to use.

In spite of my mother's thriftiness, she insisted on maintaining our pride. We were taught never to show that we were wanting. We needed to carry our heads up high (following her years of being taunted by village children). Yet, she could not comprehend the same rules in American society. Since she often tried to make do with what we had, clothes used only for one occasion was not a priority. I recall my sister's sixth grade graduation; everyone was to wear a white dress. My mother would not, or could not, afford a white dress for my sister. Instead, she found a dress that had been washed so much that all the color had come off. My mother felt this was adequate enough for one occasion, and made my sister wear it, to her great distress and humiliation.

Journey of Immigration

All immigrant families have a family saga that needs to be told to create their own family legend. These legends connect us through the generations and sustain us through life. Whether it is the story of the Pilgrims arriving on the eastern shores of Plymouth, Massachusetts or the Chinese arriving on the western shores of San Francisco, California, all immigrants share a legend of loss and abandonment of people, culture and things left behind. All start anew, in a quest on the journey for a better life. All cope with the ghosts of the past and face the trials in the present—that is, the "isms" of poverty, social class, race, gender, and age. I remember the words of my uncle, Poy Q, who said his *hey mong*, i.e., his hope, was in his children. He did not expect to live a life of leisure here in the US although he had achieved a comfortable livelihood before immigrating to America from Hong Kong. This is the journey of immigration as all make the sacrifice and transform themselves in the process toward enlightenment.

Traumatic Losses

Traumatic loss is inherent in the journey of immigration; it becomes a bondage that creates lifelong suffering "I lost my mother when I was 5." was my mother's common refrain—symbolizing a loss so traumatic that it was one of her legendary stories. This often prefaced her teachings to us about childrearing. It was the same age of her son, Sel Ming when she left him to immigrate to the US. She often reminded us of how fortunate we were to have a mother growing up so that we did not have to *sel hay* (suffer the force or breath) of a stepmother—perhaps to console herself that she was giving to us what she most missed growing up. She bore many other losses including two miscarriages brought on by working too hard, and the deaths of her first son, father and brother, by whose side she could not be.

Despite the fact that her father was largely absent in her life, she idealized his virtues—he always cared for family and for her. Without her mother, she felt pitiful growing up as she watched her aunt and stepmother deprive her of the healthy tonics and sustenance given to her cousins and half-siblings. She felt shame because other children had their mothers there to protect them. When taunted, she maintained her dignity by telling people that, "My father is overseas; he supports me and always sends me money." Her aunt countered her by saying that her father had not sent enough, thereby, creating more shame that she was unable to earn her keep. She confronts her father with this when he returned to China, only to have him become indignant because he had been dutiful in sending her money. My mother burst into tears, feeling betrayed by the shame she had been caused to feel, but grateful that her father had been loyal. Her ideal father was once again perfect.

Separation Anxiety and Abandonment

Immigrant families leave behind family, friends, home and community. The formation of Chinatowns throughout the world is the result of this separation anxiety as immigrant families seek to re-create what they gave up in their country of origin. They often perpetuate cultural practices to preserve the essence of the culture they left behind. The bondage is how they hang on to these practices long after they are given up in their countries of origin. In the need for constancy, the narrow their boundaries.

Adoptions were commonplace in China often done to replace a child who died given the high infant mortality rates, or alleviate the economic burdens of feeding another mouth given the high rates of poverty. At the same time, adoption was shameful given the premium placed on a woman's fertility, and the importance of producing sons. Adoption symbolized the abandonment and rejection. Even though adoptions were open with biological and adoptive parents often knowing one another, they were often kept secret from the adopted child for fear of losing his/her loyalty to the family. Some get stuck, like my aunt, who refused to tell her son he was adopted while his father was overseas. Even when interrogated by immigration authorities upon entry to the US at age 60+ and having to explain his conception, she preferred to admit to having an extramarital affair, and accept this "shame and loss of honor", rather than to admit under oath that she had adopted her son. This was her bondage as she struggled with her fear that her son would leave her if he discovered the truth.

There is a line of adoptions in our family that might explain the separation anxiety and feelings of abandonment experienced through the generations. My father was adopted as was his adopted father who rescued him from starvation after being abandoned by his biological father at birth after his mother died in childbirth . He was a replacement for his adoptive parents' child who died at birth. Similarly; my brother, *Sel Ming*, was adopted by my mother after her first son died at age 2. My son, Scott was also adopted.. My father's conflict over loyalty to the Lau and Lee clans and his dual relationship with both clans was lifelong. His loyalty to his adoptive parents was ever present. Yet, he was seduced by the overtures of his biological parents to bring him back despite the perception by my mother that they were exploiting his emotional bonds for monetary gain.

Some get stuck with a lifelong secret, like my aunt who refused to tell her son of his adoption. Even when interrogated by immigration authorities upon entry to the US at age 60+, she preferred to admit to having an extramarital affair, and accepting the "shame and loss of honor", rather than to admit under oath that she had adopted her son. This was her bondage as she struggled with her fear that her son would leave her if he discovered the truth.

Adoption was often a stigma in both the East and the West during earlier generations. In China, despite the close proximity and often knowledge of the whereabouts of the birth parents, it was often kept secret from the child to "prevent" favoritism toward those children who were "naturally" born. Unfortunately, these poorly kept secrets only heightened the sense of difference and alienation experienced by adopted children once they found out. These secrets also resulted in many "Cinderella complexes" among children who fear that they were adopted to explain why their parents were so mean to them. As for my father, he lived his life with two families, the Laus and the Lees; he too kept these relationships separate and "secret", fearing that he would be questioned as to his loyalty.

My older son's adoption was never a secret. Yet when my younger son Stephen was born, Scott at the age of 3 ½ , asked about "when I was in your tummy". Not wanting to traumatize him following the recent birth of a sibling, I chose to be silent with great discomfort. One day at age 5 while I was bathing the two, he once again asked, "Tell me about when I was in your tummy." This time, I told him, "You never were." In apparent shock, he said, "Do you mean you are not my mommy?" I said, "No, I am your mommy. I just did not give birth to you." Scott was very pensive that night. When I went to wake him in the morning, he related to me, "Mommy, I saw this last night. There were two mommies and they came together and became one." He gestured with his hands and showed me how he had integrated the issue of his adoption. Once considered a stigma, adoption has taken on different meaning in all cultures. When my relatives heard that I had told my son of his adoption, I was warned that this might affect his feelings of love and loyalty toward me.

The journey of immigration often involves psychological processes not unlike that of adoption. All immigrants adopt a culture. They adopt the dress, behaviors, and belie of the host culture while retaining aspects of their culture of origin. For some, it is just the exterior. For others, it is obliteration of the interior. But as my son illustrated, it is the bringing together as one, like the yin and the yang.

Survivor Guilt about those left behind

Separation and abandonment leads to survivor guilt over those who are left behind. I watched my mother struggle with her lifelong guilt over having left her son behind at the age of 5. Immigrant families of share this survivor guilt as they leave their families, their culture, and their country behind. This guilt can transcend generations as the next generation can re-create the anguish and feel compelled to make amends for the previous generation.

21 Sel Ming and family - 1981

I met my older brother, *Sel Ming,* for the first time in 1981 when he was 47 during my trip to Nanjing China with my mother. When it was time to leave after spending a week together, the pain in my mother's face of having to leave him once again is emblazed in my memory. Imagine how she and Sel Ming both recall the legendary story waking up to find her gone, and running to the train station in an attempt to catch up with her—the feelings of loss, abandonment, guilt and anger remain lifelong. Not being able to say good-bye to either Sel Ming or her dying first born son was devastating. This guilt was passed on to me when I moved to Boston—her anguish was evoked each time I left New York to return home; her guilt was passed on to me as I felt each time that I was deserting my mother once again.

Lifelong Bonds

As we traveled and shared our stories, I became aware of the lifelong bonds my mother had developed.

Obligation—A Lifelong Debt

The sharing of experiences and exchange of favors can be defining moments which result in a lifelong bond. I saw this in the unrelenting loyalty and bond between my mother and my maternal uncles, *Poy Q, Gong Q, and Hing Q* who had escaped with her from Nanjing. When we first met in Hong Kong, I did not fathom the significance of their relationship until I realized the life altering experience they had shared together.

My mother maintained contact with them through her letter writing for the 40 years while they were separated. She eventually helped to sponsor *Poy Q and Gong Q* from Hong Kong to the US, creating a lifelong a debt that he would repay. I witnessed this obligation and loyalty as my uncle, *Poy Q* would regularly honor my mother. He would bring her a chicken for her birthday, and periodically treat her to *dim sum.* Their wives helped to repay the debt as they too honored my mother. My mother also readily assisted my maternal uncle, *Hing Q,* who had emigrated to Cuba after the war, when he too wanted to come to the US. He and his wife were forever indebted to her as well .

Fulfilling a Promise

The guilt experienced by my mother for leaving *Sel Ming* behind was pervasive in our lives. She always remembered him during the holidays with monetary gifts. She followed his growth and development through their letters. Her stories were often replete with references of him. ; she tried to play the role of parent from across the ocean as she urged her brother Dai Q to watch over him, and teach him. She regularly sent them money to support his care and repayment of her debt. In trying to fulfill her promise to bring him to the US, her relationship with *Sel Ming* reflected both the bonds and bondage she felt. She and my father often argued about this drain to our meager resources. My father would get angry and accuse her relatives for being overly demanding and seeking to benefit from my mother's guilt and affections. Nothing, however, would sway her from attempting to fulfill her promise which took 50 years.

A Son's obligation—A parent's expectation

Sons are favored in Chinese families; mine was no different. My brother, Willie, became the eldest son in America—an esteemed role and burden of carrying on the family name. While he got the benefits of not doing any household chores, he also bore the burden of responsibility to protect and represent the family. He was expected to demonstrate his filial piety and obedience to my parents, but also was the one to receive the lion's share of any resources that my parents had. As daughters, our role was a secondary supporting role.

The emphasis on a son's loyalty and obligation to the family in the Chinese culture is paramount, as is a mother's influence over her son. My brother and my mother shared that special bond mother-son bond. My sister and I resented this preferential treatment, feeling my brother was spoiled while we had to clean house, cook, and do dishes. Only in adulthood did we realize how my brother envied the bonds my sister and I had shared together as females.

In Confucian tradition, defiance of parental authority is unacceptable. Parent-child conflicts over independence are often compounded within immigrant families. I saw this escalate between my father and brother as he reached adolescence. Bound by unrelenting expectations of parental obligation that my brother could not meet, he withdrew by staying out late to avoid conflict with my father, not out of fear, but out of respect and love. Angry and helpless by what he perceived as disrespect and disobedience, my father locked him out one night. My brother climbed through the second story window from the fire escape to an adjoining kitchen window risking a dangerous fall to return home.

Mother-Daughter Bonds

My mother always kept contact with her relatives and maintained the bonds. She was a prolific letter writer although she was self-conscious that her writing was not scholarly enough. She often relied on the *Hung Yeem Do Ann* (dictionary of homonyms) to find the same sounding radicals to understand a word's meaning, and find the right word. She and I had deepened our bonds with one another as we sang together, shared stories together, poured over the Chinese-English dictionaries to find words to express the new world in which I now lived—of psychology. I came to value her maternal strength.

After I started graduate school in psychology, I began to appreciate her issues anew. Or perhaps it was my journey through life, with my mother at my side that helped me to rethink my culture and my identity. As I rethought the past and met our ancestors in the present through our travels together, there were paradoxes and contradictions to reconcile. Times were changing; my mother and I were changing as we expanded our emotional and cultural bonds that transcended generational differences. In a departure from the Chinese classics of mother-son bonds, we deepened our mother-daughter bond. Together, they can create the immigration legend to transform the future.

Changing Times

Contrasting Images

I have images of my *Cherng Por* (Maternal Great Aunt) talk with amazement of how her grandchildren greet her with a kiss as it is done in Western cultures—she said she has learned to accept it when they "suck your face" (kiss her). Toisanese elders were more likely to grab your hands or stroke your face as a sign of endearment.

These contrasting images are seen when I enter the homes of Toisanese immigrants who have lived in Chinatown for decades. While deeply connected with their communities, they rarely see or talk with someone white not from Chinatown. Entering their homes is like a time warp, not much different from what they left in China. They remain insular in their lifestyle, contrasting dramatically with that their children and grandchildren who are quick to adopt the toys and trappings of our digital and technological society—most prominently cell phones and computers.

These contrasting images mirror the contrasts between generations, and between East and West as immigrant families adjust and develop their unique and positive bicultural identities. These contrasting images reflect differences in world views (Kluckhohn & Strodtbeck, 1961), a Value-Orientation Model (Ibrahim, 1985) which suggests that cultures differ along dimensions of time, human activity, social relationships, relationship of people to nature which influence their behavior and values in life. For example, the Asian emphasis on modesty and indirectness contrasts with the Western emphasis on assertiveness and directness. Asian values based on Confucian principles--emphasizing hierarchy and order contrasts with Taoism principles--emphasizing equality and fluidity. Asian cultures view power and authority with benevolence as opposed to it being dictatorial. They do not suppress emotions, but avoid public displays of emotions. Emphasizing the differences rather than comparing them to assign a value is important to minimize pejorative meanings attached to different cultural expressions. Table 2 compares these differences between Asian and Western worldviews.

Table 2. Asian vs. Western Values and Worldviews

Asian Values	Western Values
Family/Group oriented	Individual oriented
Extended family	Nuclear family
Multiple parenting	Couple parenting
Primary relationship based on parent-child bond	Primary relationship based on marital bond
Emphasis on interpersonal relationship	Emphasis on self-fulfillment and self-development
Status and relationships determined by age and role in family	Status achieved by individual's efforts
Well-defined family members' roles	Flexible family members' roles
Favoritism toward males	Increasing opportunities for females
Authoritarian orientation	Democratic orientation
Suppression of public displays of emotions	Free expression of emotions
Fatalism/karma	Personal control over the environment
Harmony with nature	Mastery over nature
Cooperative orientation	Competitive orientation
Spiritualism	Materialism/consumerism
Past, present, future	Present, future orientation

<table>
<tr><td>orientation</td><td></td></tr>
</table>

Status of Women

Coinciding with the Women's Movement of the 1960s challenging the inequitable roles of women, and steeped in Chinese cultural tradition which honored the status of men, we began to question whether a marriage should be premised on the subservience of women to men. We became annoyed with my mother for being so subservient to my father's needs. We would get angry about her constant sacrifice at the cost of her own needs. We would get angry that she would put others before herself. We would urge her to stand up for herself. We simply could not understand how difficult it was for her to transcend the Chinese belief of maternal sacrifice—that a woman's honor was her virtue—not to be selfish, but to be generous and nurturing leading others to honor you with respect and gifts.

Yet there were glimmers of how bold my mother could be. A defining moment occurred as we were walking home from the subway one day. My father suddenly turned to her and chided her, "Don't walk so close to me, it doesn't look nice!" He was expecting my mother to walk 10 paces behind him as women were expected to do in China as a sign of deference to their husbands. Suddenly, my mother got furious and stood up to him saying, "I'm your wife! I'm not a prostitute! What do you mean it doesn't look nice?" Although known for his violent temper, my father did not protest. He must have forgotten that times have changed, and that he was no longer in China. He sheepishly walked on, made aware that he needed to adjust to changing times about the roles of men and women. And so, my mother challenged the male dominant norms of the time.

A Mother's Pride

I became a psychologist. When I decided to go on to graduate school, I remember trying to explain to my mother what psychology was. Given my limited vocabulary in Chinese and her limited understanding of the humanities, I tried to explain that I was studying the mind. After several attempts using simple words to describe an esoteric field, my mother's face suddenly lit up with delight; "Oh, I understand. You are going to be a neurosurgeon".

Although my mother believed in education, graduations simply did not seem important because it was an American custom. Although she supported our education and we always knew she was proud of our accomplishments, she refused to participate in any school functions or parent events because of her inability to speak English. Her excuse was always, "I don't understand what they're saying; I'd just sit there like an idiot or a crazy person."

When I published my first book, I gave my mother a copy knowing full well she would not be able to read it. She looked at me puzzled, and as always protested that she could not read English: "so what was the point?" I felt foolish until I shared this story with my co-author. He had done the same with his Spanish speaking mother. He told me how he had given the book to his mother, and before she could protest, simply told her to keep it on her coffee table for company. We both knew the importance of having a mother's pride in our accomplishments. And though our mothers could not read English and could not always comprehend the nature of our accomplishments, their pride and pleasure were always communicated through the simple gestures of showing off our accomplishments to friends and family. These were the images that sustained us.

Power of the Unspoken Word

Chinese families often use indirectness and are nonverbal in their communication. Some things in families never get spoken--There are just things we knew. My mother would always say, "You should not have to be told!" We knew our parents expected us to respect them. We knew how important it was to be Chinese. We knew the importance of family. Perhaps it was the way in which my parents looked at us, or the sternness with which they spoke. We might boldly say in defiance that we had a choice not to do something, or that we had a mind of our own especially as teenagers when we believed we knew everything. But, we knew deep down that there were things we could never do because of the power of the unspoken word. We simply did not challenge our parents' authority.

When cultural taboo did not permit something to be spoken, nonverbal and somatic symptoms expressed the unspoken. The stress of poverty and immigration manifested itself in somatic symptoms in both my parents. I remember a period in my mother's life when she began to develop many physical and somatic ailments as she tried to cope with the hardships in her life. She would threaten suicide, in typical Chinese fashion and exasperation. We usually felt it was a means of controlling us. She would threaten to jump off the Brooklyn Bridge, but say she was waiting for the next milestone in our lives (e.g., to see us married, to see us graduate). At another point, she developed bleeding ulcers which were life threatening from her years of sacrifice and internalizing her distress. Having to endure poverty; leaving behind her eldest son, and not being there for her father's death were stress inducers. Most of all, she was angry over my father's domineering personality and bad temper, but felt that a dutiful and virtuous wife should not complain. According to Confucian tradition, sacrifice was to have its rewards; my mother was becoming disenchanted. Her illness and threats were unspoken ways of telling us this.

My father was a proud man. Despite his violent temper, he was unable to speak about his vulnerabilities. His periodic outbreaks of dermatitis spoke for him. Compelled to fulfill his provider and protector roles as father and husband, these outbreaks of dermatitis provided the means of relief. When his dermatitis inflamed his legs, he was no longer able to stand for the long hours of laundry work. When he went to work as a dishwasher in a restaurant, the detergent water led to inflammation of his dermatitis on his hands. Tough economic times strained the relationship between my parents. My father became more volatile, and more rigid in his ways. He vented his frustrations on my mother as he felt more trapped by the absence of choices before him. Although having a bad temper is not a valued trait in Chinese culture, it is sanctioned as part of a man's character. He resorted to smoking and alcohol as two vices that helped to numb the pain. He smoked at least a pack a day, and insisted on a shot of whiskey with his dinner. He developed emphysema in his later years that consumed most of his lungs; yet, he boldly refused to give up "his only two enjoyments of his life".

An Awakening

Transformation

Like Monkey King, Chinese immigrants made their journey to the West and were transformed as they traveled their fantastic adventures. As they immigrated to the shores of *Fa Kay* (flowered flag) or *Mei Kuo* (Beautiful Country), as America was called, they too submitted to the 81 trials. Their journey was captured in the letters sent to families in China—storytelling. These stories described the unimaginable: gold in the streets, riches of Westerners, and luxurious living. These stories were made believable by the money that accompanied these letters to starving families in Guangzhou, China. Women and children with husbands and fathers in *gnoy yerng* (overseas) bragged about and enjoy the material comforts provided by their husbands and fathers.

But after the letter writing, the Chinese immigrant men would congregate in their family clan associations in *Mei Kuo* and tell other stories—stories of Chinatowns burning, working the dusty gold mines long abandoned by the whites, cleaning the dirty laundry of the *bak gul* (white devils), and facing the racist behavior. On Sundays, their only day of rest, they shared stories of how the *bak gul* will never let you forget that your skin is yellow, how the land of equal opportunity was only open to whites. They shared stories of starvation here in America, of having to sleep on hard ironing boards instead of beds, of toiling in the laundry 12 hour days,

6 days a week. They shared their dreams of returning home to China to retire as rich men. Their enlightenment was but a vision; their transformation a dream. They reminisced and dreamed of the endless beauty of China, a place where lychee nuts grew in such abundance you picked up as they fell off the trees, a place where they would be honored for being old. Out of these stories grew the immigration myths—a mix of truth and embellishment.

Asian American Pride

There was an awakening of Asian American pride in Chinatown during the 1960s and 1970s. The leaders were younger men and women in their 20s and 30s, many aligned with the Civil Rights movement and the Asian American movement; they showed a force of strength as they created Chinatown's social welfare programs. Soon there were factions who competed for community control. Younger groups challenged the longstanding power of the Chinese Consolidated Benevolent Association, made up of Chinese elders from all of the family clan associations, and historically known as the power base of Chinatown.

There was now a new middle class of Chinese Americans. Families from Hong Kong immigrated to join their families in New York. The new second generation *jook sing* (American born Chinese) were now adults. They no longer accepted the injustices bore by their parents; they had the language and education to challenge it. A new Asian American culture was born. Having grown up in an urban environment, they dressed fashionably in Western garb and stood out in stark contrast to the old-timers – the elderly Chinese women with knitted hats, layers of sweaters, and *men knop* (Chinese style, down filled vests) or the elderly Chinese men with their white shirts, buttoned cardigan sweaters and caps, always smoking a cigarette.

Newer immigrants from Taiwan, Fuzhou, and other parts of China now filled the streets of New York's Chinatown. The number of street peddlers who sold vegetables and trinkets at unbeatable prices multiplied; they could because they had no overhead and only wanted to survive. Suddenly there were Asian youth gangs, with origins in Hong Kong that terrorized the community. Family clan associations seeking to gain control of Chinatown often supported these gangs to protect their economic and business interests in the form of the many gambling houses that they owned. The Flying Dragons, the gang supported by Hip Sing clan association, "owned Pell Street"(Kinkead, 1991); the Ghost Shadows, the gang supported by On Leong clan association, "owned" Mott Street. The gangs were the muscle for the Chinese elders to collect debts and extortion money. Suddenly we had Chinese preying on Chinese, extorting Chinatown businesses for protection money; Chinatown was no longer the safe haven.

Confucius Plaza—The end of an Era

In front of Confucius Plaza, a publicly funded housing project with mixed income housing where my mother lived in the last two decades of her life stands a ten-foot bronze statue of the sage Confucius. This was a present from the Chinese Consolidated Benevolent Association. It is a different era now. Cher Long Fong, the Lau clan association, is now defunct. My father has passed away as have many of the men of his generation. Families moved away. Few were willing to pay the fee to maintain this association since they were no longer congregating there. Most men had families now. The small clan associations were largely gone; in their place were social service agencies.

Many more elderly women now congregate at the associations created by the social welfare programs, or at the Mulberry Street Park on sunny, warm days. My mother used to hang out there as she had done decades earlier at the clan associations. These women now exchange stories of the hardships in the garment factories that had since replaced the laundries. These "sweatshops" provide a sewing machine and a chair; women work piecework in a production line, getting a few cents a seam; many would need to work 12 hour days to make $200/week. There is no minimum wage and minimal protection from safety hazards. The lowest paid workers, mostly women in their 60s and 70s, no longer as swift or as skilled, are the thread cutters; they snip threads from finished garments and are paid pennies per garment.

The younger immigrant women with children often cannot not afford babysitters and have to leave their children home alone after school. I remember the stories of my Poy Kim's (maternal aunt's) niece, So Lan; who talked of playing in the stairwell landing outside the garment factory after school while waiting for her mother to finish work. There were no toys; at one point, they played in a large box discarded from a delivery of garments. Life in America was supposed to have been a better life, but we see families in bondage, imprisoned by the economic realities of our society.

Rethinking The Past

As we look back, there are stories of regret and remorse. I remember stories about *Ah Sam Gung*, (Number Three Great Uncle) who slaved away for 40 years selling 10 cent cups of coffee and one dollar meals; he always managed to send money back to his wife in China while living in America under squalid conditions. Believing that *Ah Sam Gung* was a rich man in America (since he never corrected this myth), his wife treated her friends and relatives in China to generous banquets and gifts. Left by her husband as a young bride in her 20s, she joined him as an elderly woman in her 60s in the US; she lived the remaining 15 years of her life in misery, crying and chastising herself for her spendthrift ways while she now lived in near poverty conditions. She cried daily over how she and her husband had lost the best years of their lives apart.

Another uncle came to America on his own at the age of 15. He found work to support himself, built a restaurant business, and raised a family; but he never saw his parents again—a fact he bemoaned. He could not bring himself to talk about this even as a grandparent as it brought back such intense feelings of pain and loss. As I listened to these stories, I turned to look at my son, then 14, unable to imagine his making it in another country on his own without family supports, or to bear the thought of my never seeing him again for the rest of my life.

Despite her peasant origins and sixth grade education, my mother was willing to change with the times. Although she was confined to Chinatown, she eagerly sought to expand her horizons. When we went shopping, she would drop her chin and roll her eyes in shock at the high prices, and remind us of the times when a loaf of bread cost only 5 cents. While she did not understand the fashion or the music of the times, she was always amused and tolerant. She would laugh and shake her head in disbelief at the new fashions that featured torn and faded jeans. When my nephew Greg was living with me, it was the fashion to wear un-ironed, wrinkled clothes. After having done his laundry one evening, he stuffed them into a basket to get the perfect set of wrinkles. My mother viewed these wrinkles with the eyes of a laundrywoman and neatly pressed shirts; she "took pity" on him and proceeded to iron his shirts for him. Ever the respectful grandchild, my nephew dared not tell her that he wanted them wrinkled. When my mother found the clothes she had neatly ironed wrinkled up in the basket, she was confused. She came to me asking for an explanation. When I explained to her that this was the fashion, she shook her head in disbelief.

Freedom: Learning from My Mother's Voice

Warrior Lessons (Eng, 1999), a book about Chinese American women, talks of "fitting in" not as an exercise in self-hatred, but as a coping mechanism for self-love. The lessons are to recognize the different journey that Chinese American immigrant families take. Our differences are visible and influence how we see and are seen. We must decide the images we want to communicate about who we are, and how our behaviors will be perceived. As we challenge prevailing stereotypes and expectations which constrain us, will we losing our credibility? Will our differences be a distraction from the substance of our words and deeds? As an example, Whites can choose to express themselves by dressing in Asian ethnic garb--it becomes a conversation piece. When Asians choose to do the same, it is viewed as fitting the mode. Warrior Lessons describes how an Asian's inquisitive smile is viewed as one of apparent compliance by whites, but used as defiance and rebellion by Asians—it is a power issue. Warrior Lessons urges us to understand these differences and contradictions for us to find our freedom.

What do we learn from this journey? The context is changed but the stories remain the same. As my mother changed with the times, she found freedom as she found her voice, and I learned from my mother's voice. I begin to think of the stories my mother told and retold. Now I hear them differently. Where I saw dependency before, I now saw her bold and fierce spirit. Where I felt annoyance and impatience, I now appreciate her plight of leaving her home, her son, family and culture. Where I saw contradiction in her obedience to my father vs. her challenging of society, I now see them reconciled. In writing her story, I create her legend, and preserve her voice for our children and grandchildren to form our bonds together.

Children are Like Birds

I often remember the words of my mother. She often became pensive and sad after recounting some of her stories, and would exclaim, "Children are like birds; they grow up and fly away!" During these times, there was little I could say to dissuade her. We were always too quick to dismiss her musings especially when our contrasting viewpoints led to disagreement and frustration. My mother would then say, "Just wait until you become a parent, you'll see." These memories and my mother's words were defining moments and mirrors to the future.

Through Our Eyes

My mother saw America through our eyes—through her children. Since she spoke little English, we generally translated for her and escorted her to places outside Chinatown. Like most Chinese immigrants, her fear of mainstream society was pervasive

As she viewed America through our eyes, we viewed China through hers. She would sing the praises of Chinese culture—"Chinese culture is one of thousands of years compared to American culture which is only a few hundred. She would describe the splendor of Chinese artifacts—the beauty of Guilin, the magnificence of the Great Wall. She would call my attention to Chinese inventions as forerunners of modern technology. I became interested in the abacus that she used to compute the laundry prices; I would watch her use this rack of beads and rapidly compute complex arithmetic simply by moving the beads. She taught me the practice exercise accompanied by a song used as a pneumonic for addition and subtraction; it is not unlike the alphabet song familiar to most American children.

Her Chinese pride was prominent as we shared these times together. The importance of "having face" was reinforced so often from her indignity about the occupation of Shanghai to deceitful efforts of her father-in-law to discredit her honor. It played out in our day-to-day interactions in the importance of maintaining dignity of ourselves (having face) to that of showing respect for others (giving face). As a case in point, many immigrants experienced starvation prior to coming to the U.S. so the abundance of food is highly significant. Though we were frugal on a daily basis, we were always sure to have excess food whenever guests were invited to dinner. This was intended to demonstrate our respect and honor of our guests, and to maintain our dignity by showing our plentiful resources. We were always careful not to appear greedy or act if we had nothing to eat (i.e., beggars) by being too eager to dive into a meal; we were always taught to wait for our elders or honored guests to begin.

As children, we viewed these practices with disdain and bewilderment. While we understood the pride, we could not understand the practices which made little sense or no longer served a useful purpose with the abundance of food in America—yet, Chinese immigrants still held strongly to these practices.

One defining moment of the importance of Asian pride stands out in my mind. A neighborhood parent came to my mother to complain about my behavior after her daughter and I had had a fight. I have long forgotten the reason for that fight. All I remember was my mother slapping me across my face upon hearing the neighbor's complaint to my dismay, shame and anger. Even the neighbor was embarrassed and quickly suggested that it was OK. After the neighbor left, my mother explained to me that she did not think I was wrong, but did not want the neighbor to think that she had not done a good job as a parent in disciplining me. This was her way of showing that she was a good parent. She did not want to "lose face."

We Shall Not Forget

As my mother aged, she tended to her plants and picked up knitting when she was not visiting with friends and relatives or exercising. She knitted hats galore with the signature quality of so many of her contemporaries. She was always proud of her creations, giving them as gifts to friends, relatives, and us in her continuing efforts to demonstrate her generosity. She had come a long way from the days when her ulcers and my father's dermatitis symbolized how much stress and how helpless she felt. She had accomplished her work of raising her children, and remained proud.

My mother had dreams that paralleled the idealism of the Civil Rights Movement and the Women's Movement of the 1960s. These were times of great transformation in the fight for freedom, and the images of that era are embodied in my mother's words. I hear her voice, and her wisdom as loudly as the day they were spoken; they sooth and guide my actions. I am constantly reminded of her stories, and her heeding that "We shall not forget" the suffering, the pain, and the challenges of those who came before.

CHAPTER 8: LESSONS FOR THE NEXT GENERATION

The mythology and symbols of Part I connect us with the past to guide us toward the future. The intergenerational saga of one family in Part II examines their journey of immigration—about biculturalism, survival and striving, loss and abandonment, bonds and bondage. This saga celebrates mothers and women, families and culture as the sustaining forces that guides us on the journey of immigration. We caution against the myths and symbols that put immigrant families in bondage where they end up in the ghettos of the mind or place—even when social and financial conditions no longer limit their options. The environment can reinforce negative messages that entrap us, perpetuate the ghosts that haunt us, and put us in bondage.

We urge you toward the symbols and messages that empower and bond. We urge you to tell your story and create your family legend to enable you to connect with your hidden strengths, to empower and give you voice. In telling their story, families can heal from the trauma of the immigration experience, strengthen their intergenerational bonds, and change their narrative from images of hopelessness that victimize and oppress to bonding images that promote growth. It can facilitate the expression of affect and the resolution of conflict. It is a developmental process and a journey.

We end with some lessons to be learned, that each person can use to tell their family saga. The lessons identify the problem and bondage message, the lesson, and the action steps needed to change the narrative to a bonding image.

Lesson 1: Navigate the developmental process of Immigration

Problem: Immigration is about loss and separation from family, community, and culture. It is a traumatic process with guilt and anger over abandonment often lifelong.

Bondage Image: Chinese women in Bound Feet

Lesson: Bondage—As immigrants try to simply "Get over it!" or deny the  reality of their circumstances, they remain in bondage, and often create idealized stories rather talk about the painful realities. The lesson is that the immigration experience is a developmental task. Whether we use our faith or accept our fate, immigrants need to acknowledge their normal feelings of loss and abandonment, guilt and anger. They need to acknowledge the trauma and learn to mourn. Evoke the bonding images to push you toward your dreams and message of hope and freedom.

Bonding Image: the Statue of Liberty as a symbol of the American Dream to remind us of why we came and to wish us speedy passage.

Lesson 2. Find the Woman Warrior in you

Problem: Images of women put them in bondage when gender role expectations for women are to be subservient to men. Contrasting images of Asian women as exotic China dolls—to be played with, or damsels in distress needing to be rescued renders them as helpless victims. Moreover, the complexity of face, shame, and modesty within the Chinese culture further reinforces perceptions of Asian women as weak and self-denigrating.

Bondage Image: Miss Saigon in the popular Western depiction of Asian women as naïve, modest, and subservient to men rendering them pitiful vs. contrasting image of women being cunning, conniving, and immoral, thereby deserving of mistreatment .

Lesson: Celebrate women's strength and pride as they face challenges in a paradoxical world. The contrasting images of women belie an underlying fear of women's hidden power. Asian women must confront these images to avoid being stereotyped as exotic and passive, and challenge the racism and sexism that keeps them in bondage. Our stories need to end with admiration, not pity for the heroine. Become the Woman Warrior, and use your sword to fight the ghosts of the past, and the barricades of racism and sexism which block and silence us.

Bonding Image: Strength and pride of the Woman Warrior

Lesson 3. Find the Hidden power of the Moon Goddess

Problem: As in Lesson 2, the contrasting images of women put them into bondage.

Bondage Image: Lady Chang-O, lives in the Moon. After stealing the elixir of immortality from Houyi, her husband, she floated to the moon and remains there in isolation.

Lesson: Celebrate woman's connectedness and the fertilizing power of the

Moon Goddess as guardian of the waters. The birth of each new moon symbolize that invisible hidden power of "bringing forth from within"—or feminine creation. It is women's connectedness in immigrant families that nurtured and healed, and formed the bonds that held families and communities together. Avoid the bondage images of dependency and emotionality that render you isolated and trapped.

Bonding Image: Celebrate the Moon Goddess as the powerful, benevolent, forgiving, and nurturing mother.

Lesson 4:Achieve a Positive Identity

Problem: Developing a positive identity is a developmental process. External perceptions and expectations of Asians such as "the perpetual foreigner" can rupture that process creating doubt and confusion.

Bondage Image: In the beginning of time, all was chaos…Chaos was shaped like a hen's egg. Always being told to choose: "Be American!"

or "Give up your traditional ways" can put you into bondage by trying to be what you cannot.

Lesson: Asian Americans need to be vigilant about identifying the stereotypic perceptions and expectations which constrain them. Asian immigrant families must develop a yin/yang balance between Eastern and Western cultures, and develop a positive bicultural identity. Evoke the Asian images of the Phoenix rising from the South, the Snake from the North, the Dragon from the East, and the Tiger from the West to protect, nurture and give you strength, and to bring happiness, health, and fertility.

Bonding Image: White Tiger to protect and four directions of protection, power and strength

Lesson 5: Deal with the Contradictions of Culture

Problem: Contrasting worldviews and values between Asian and Western cultures can cause conflict, contradiction, and confusion.

Bondage Image: Demons which blind you to the truth.

Lesson: Cultures hold different worldviews which shape identity, one's decisions and goals in life. Keeping these identities separate can help to preserve the integrity of each. Learn to live with contrasts and contradictions of culture. Engage in a bidirectional process to bridge different cultures, and use constant translation and cultural humility to appreciate the differences.

Bonding Image: Achieve a Yin-Yang balance in developing your bicultural identity.

Lesson 6: Find your Voice

Problem: Our faith sustains us on our journey of life; or is it our fate that makes us persevere in our travels. Yet, many immigrants get trapped by the enormous guilt and sadness that bury them. Oppression and powerlessness often results from Persistent racism and sexism, and

other injustices often put them in bondage of oppression and powerlessness.

Bondage Image: The three wise Monkeys who "see no evil, hear no evil, speak no evil" can lead you to turn a blind eye to truth. It can put you us into bondage by acquiescing and complying with injustice.

Lesson: You must find your voice. The task for all immigrants is to restore, to heal, and to bond. Do not forget the suffering and pain to get there. It is a dynamic process of transformation as important as reaching the end of the journey.

Bonding Image: Remember Monkey King who

needed to discern truth from fiction, and to endure 81 trials before he reached enlightenment.

Lesson 7: Establishing Intergenerational Bonds

Problem: Confucianism prescribes a hierarchical order to gender and family relationships in order to create social order and stability. However, these precepts, e.g., honoring your elders, can pose dilemmas as children strive for independence, negotiate relationships in a bicultural society.

Bondage Image: Allowing our family "ghosts" to haunt us as we relive the past, live in shame, or fight the battles we cannot win.

Lesson: Drawing on extended family relationships and intergenerational  bonds to heal, nurture and sustain you. Avoid the bondage of myths and practices that limit your opportunities and constrain you. Strive for balance and harmony as in a perfectly executed Chinese banquet—achieving the balance and harmony of dishes, color, taste, texture, and ingredients which all complement one another and create a harmonious whole. Recognize and appreciate the interdependence that sustains these intergenerational bonds'

Bonding Image: The harmony and balance of a perfectly executed Chinese banquet.

Lesson 8: Tell your Story to Heal and to Bond

Problem: All immigrant families have a saga of the trauma, loss and separation, and the trials of their journey.

Bondage Image: Headband of Monkey King controls him by giving him severe headaches when he is errant.

 Lesson: Tell your story of your journey. It is a healing process to remember what came before. It is a bonding process to share it with others. It is a nurturing process much like the herbal chicken soup made by Chinese mothers to nurture and sooth your body and soul.

Bonding Image:: Herbal Chicken Soup

Lesson 9: Create your Family Legend

Problem: Many immigrant parents fear their children will forget their saga of struggle and suffering.

Bondage Images: Embellishing the stories with fantasy to maintain face or deny the pain only puts you into bondage.

Lesson: Write your family saga of your journey of immigration, and create your family legend. Draw on the cultural symbols and rituals in your life. It is the bitter that makes us know the sweet. It is the cold that makes us know what is hot. It is the spicy that lets us know what is mild. Create your family legend to preserve the memories so that we do not forget, and build the bonds to support you. It is a journey of transformation and of enlightenment at the end.

Bonding Image: Journey to the West

CHAPTER 9 THE FUTURE

Symbols and Images

Number 9 (ghew) in Chinese symbolizes longevity and immortality. Thus, it is appropriate to end this book with Chapter 9 for our future and for the - generations to follow. It is the bond to be sustained through time and the family legend.

I see images of old Toisanese Chinese ladies in knitted hats and sweaters, wearing layers of clothing to keep them warm. Their fashion consists of dark earth tone colors to be modest, small multi-color flowery prints to give some life, but not to be too flamboyant, and sensible shoes to help them make their journey.

I see images of old Toisanese Chinese men sitting around mahjong tables, talking story. Their stories support one another's anguish and struggle. It diminishes the suffering. Only among themselves can they admit to the harsh realities of life in America. These images speak to loss and trauma.   But this is the journey of immigration—loss and abandonment; feeling unwelcome in a strange new world.

Some choose to deny their painful experiences. They push them out of consciousness. Some dream of a more idyllic China. As they huddled together amidst barren and squalid surroundings recounting their endless stories, the sojourners omitted the outrages and struggles of living in a hostile and racist America in their letters to their wives and families. They remained proud; they embellished their stories and sent home money. This was the 20th century.

Today, in the 21st century, China is an emergent world power; political relations between China and the US have improved. Economic conditions in China have improved. Even those in the rural villages have cellphones and internet access. No longer do they wait months for a letter. Second and third Chinese Americans are largely educated professionals and American citizens. Many can now afford to travel, and return to visit their ancestral villages in China. There are now four Chinatowns in New York City—but there is diversity in the population and fusion in the food. Chinese immigrants are drawn to Chinatown by choice, but immigrate from Fuzhou, Szechuan, and many parts of China, no longer from Toisan or depending on the seafaring cities for transport. The diaspora of Chinese include immigrants from Taiwan, Malaysia, and Singapore. Chinese food, once known as the comfort foods of old Toisan or the modified versions of chop suey and chow mein for tourists seeking the exotic, has reached new heights in their variety from Cantonese, Szechuan, Fuzhou, Malaysian to the fusion with Japanese, Cuban, and Western cuisines.

Reclaiming the Past

As we conclude this journey, it is time to move toward the future. Immigrant families must reclaim their past. They must travel an arduous journey and endure the trials of oppression, acculturation, poverty, and undergo transformation before they reach enlightenment, i.e., empowerment. And so, we completed our journey in the next generation as my husband Gene, my brother Willie and I traveled west to reach East We returned to China to visit our ancestral villages in Toisan in 2013 and 2015. This was the completion of a cycle as my mother would have said. We were connecting with our roots and completing our parents' dream to *fan hong san* (return to Tang Mountain as China was called).

My mother told me stories growing up about how idyllic village life was with fresh longan fruit ready to be picked off the trees when in season or of the majestic and unparalleled beauty of China. Or she would describe the village outhouses with no flushing toilets, and the perils of falling in between the slats. In our travels, my mother would introduce me to friends or relatives who lived just across from their door, on the same *hong*, or in the same village.

My parents made great sacrifices to support their families and relatives in China despite living in poverty themselves. I recall overhearing them talking about letters from relatives in China always asking for money. They would become incensed with the unreasonable demands, but my father nevertheless acquiesced to his brother's requests for money to marry his nephew, or repair their roof. My father never forgot his loyalty and lifelong obligations to the Lee family clan.

Just as we did not have a clue about village life, they did not have a clue of our city life in America. To the villagers, all who returned from *gnow yerng* were rich and were expected to return bearing gifts and host a banquet for the entire village as a sign of respect. This is what my parents did in their 1972 return to China

Most people in China today are no longer starving, and have a reasonable middle class life. They no longer expect the handouts from their "rich" relatives in America. Many ancestral villages, however, are depleted as families have reunited in the US. The younger generation have largely left the villages for jobs in the cities; few return. Some villages now resemble ghost towns with a largely senior population—usually the grandparents caring for grandchildren whose parents are working in the cities.

Return to Our Ancestral Villages

23 Oong Ben Loong Village Gate

Oong Been Loong Toon in 49-50—that was our ancestral village of the Lee clan in Toisan, China where my father was born in 1903. The name of our village was imprinted in our minds by my parents. Whenever we were asked, "Where are you from?" upon meeting new Chinese relatives or friends, we dutifully recited *Oong Been Long, 49-50* without the faintest idea what we were talking about.

My father always told stories about his youth in the village, of being a spoiled first born son. He was reputed for his spirited rebelliousness and proudly told us of how he was punished by being hung by his feet from the Banyan tree in front of the village community center.

22 Banyan Tree with first cousins

Upon arriving at the village gate, we were shocked to be greeted my two first cousins—sons of my father's two younger brothers, and later joined by the wife of a third first cousin. With some suspicion, we conversed until my cousin recounted the legendary story of my father being hung by his feet under the Banyan tree. Although we had only been using honorific titles, my cousin's wife suddenly asked to verify the names of all my siblings. When she brought out a picture of my father's 70th birthday sent to her by my mother more than 30 years ago, our identities were confirmed. What a shock to find cousins we had thought perished during WWII. What a reunion!

In our tour of the village, the *hongs* were these narrow streets between the homes. All the homes were architecturally the same. Gone were the water buffaloes and pigs my parents used to talk about. A chicken coop still stands outside my cousin's house with a live chicken living in the house to lay eggs. The rice paddies are replaced by the peanut farming. Men still gathered under the large banyan tree to socialize or play mah-jong when not working in the fields.

The interiors of the homes have not changed after almost 100 years. All the village houses have the same configuration of a central living area with a a kitchen at the back and a loft above sleeping or storage; a bedroom on either side for the

24 Hong- village street

parents and children exist. This would have accommodated the extended family in the past if the oldest son were to marry. My parents would have occupied one of the two bedrooms with my grandparents so I was told

We held the traditional ceremony of lighting incense to honor my ancestors, and shared a meal with my cousins as we traded stories of the past 50 years. My cousin talked of my father's generosity and loyalty as he financed the repair of the roof and his marriage.

25 Village living room

26 Village kitchen

27 Village Bedroom

My Mother's Village: Xiangang (Hen Gong) in Kaiping (Hoiping), China

28 Kaiping Community Center

We took a trip to visit *Hen Gong in Hoiping,* a village several hours away, the birth place of our mother where she lived till she was 14. The architecture here showed their western influence and historical significance of being financed by overseas Chinese in America who sent money back to build these monuments and homes.

With little information other than my maternal grandfather's name and the name of my mother's village, we were shocked to find not only her village, but also the genealogy book maintained by the village elders with the help of the local Chief of Police who personally escorted us to the village to meet with the Village Mayor and District Leader. What a shock and pleasant surprise to find the names of our grandfather, uncles and male cousins, who were all in America, recorded there. My mother's name was not listed as the custom declared that women left the family when they married.

29 Kaiping Village leaders and Chief of Police

Coming Together

I started with the voice of the ancestors and Chinese scholars. Through my mother's voice—a Toisanese grandmother, she made her Journey to the West. In our later years, my mother and I made our journey together as we traveled the world, shared our struggles and our joys. By the age of 84, she had achieved the blessing of having 100 children (including grandchildren, great-grandchildren, nieces, nephews, and all their offspring). She was a loving mother. She died tragically in a car accident, suffering in her death as she did in life. As we went through her effects, we were reminded of how she lived, of how much she gave. There were gathered, gifts never used because they were too precious open; gifts never given because there was a tomorrow for her to look forward to. Unfinished business; she was frugal to the end; generous till she died.

Our consolation was she knew she was loved. The scores of people that came to pay their respects at her funeral was testimony to the person. She would have felt that her life was worth living. For she had achieved the greatest honor a woman could have—to be respected and appreciated, to be loved by her family. She died as she lived; a martyr and a hero. She often felt insignificant in the world; but she was significant in her life, to her family. We will not forget her journey.

REFERENCES

Barlow, T. E., with Bjorge, G. J. (Eds.) (1989) I Myself am a Woman. Selected Writings of Ding Ling. Boston: Beacon Press.

Bettelheim, B. (1976) The Uses of Enchantment: The meaning and importance of fairy tales. NY: Alfred A. Knopf.

Bierlein, J. F. (1994) Parallel Myths. NY: Ballantine Books, 1994.

Campbell, J. (1949) Hero with a Thousand Faces. NJ: Princeton University Press.

Chang, I. C. (1968) Chinese Fairy Tales. NY: Schocken Books.

Eng, P. (1999) Warrior Lessons: An Asian American's Journey into Power. NY: Pocket Books.

Gibson, C. (1996) Signs and symbols: An illustrated guide to their meaning and origins. New York: Barnes & Nobles Books.

Harding, M. E. (1971) Woman's Mysteries: Ancient and Modern. Boston: Shambhala Publications, Inc.

Heuscher, J. E. (1974) A Psychiatric Study of Myths and Fairy Tales. Ill: Chas. C. Thomas.

Ibrahim, F.A. (1985) Effective Cross-Cultural Counseling and Psychotherapy: A Framework. The Counseling Psychologist, 12, 625-638.

Kim, E. H. (1981) Visions and Fierce Dreams: A Commentary on the Works of Maxine Hong Kingston. Amerasia Journal, 8(2), 145-162.

Kim, J. (1981) The process of Asian American identity development: A study of Japanese-American women's perceptions of their struggle to achieve personal identities as Americans of Asian ancestry. Dissertation Abstracts International, 42, 155 1A. (University Microfilms No. 81-18080)

Kingston, M.H. (1989) The Woman Warrior: Memoirs of a Girlhood among Ghosts. NY: Random House.

Kinkead, G. (1991) Chinatown: A Portrait of a Closed Society. NY: HarperCollins Publishers.

Kluckhohn, F. R. & Strodtbeck, F. L. (1961) Variations in Value Orientations. Evanston, IL: Row, Patterson & Co.

Kristeva, J. (1986) About Chinese Women. NY: Marion Boyars.

Lam, A. (1996) Drinking Tiger Soup. Pacific News Service.

Lee, E. (1997) Working with Asian Americans: A guide for clinicians. NY: The Guilford Press.

Lion Dance http://a2amas.com/liondance/ Retrieved June 2002.

Loo, C. M., & Yu, C. Y. (1984) Pulse on San Francisco's Chinatown: Health service utilization and health status. Amerasia, 11:1, 55-73.

Madame Butterfly. http://www.culturevulture.net/Opera/Butterfly.htm Retrieved June 2002.

McDermott, J. F., & Lum, K. Y. (1980) Star Wars: The Modern Developmental Fairy Tale. Bulletin of the Menninger Clinic, 44(4), 381-390.

Monkey King http://www.china-on-site.com/pages/comic/comiccatalog1.php Retrieved May 2002.

Okonogi as quoted by Tatara, 1980. In Chin, J. C., Liem, J. H., Ham, M.D-C. & Hong, G. (1993) Transference and Empathy in Asian American Psychotherapy: Cultural Values and Treatment Needs. Westport, CT: Praeger Publishers, p.25.

Romance of the Three Kingdoms. http://www.3kingdoms.net/intro.htm Retrieved May 2002

Scott, D. H. (1980) Chinese Popular Literature and the Child. Chicago: American Library Association.

Simpson, C. S. (2001) Crouching Tiger: the Rebirth of Myth. The Chronicle of Higher Education, March 23, 2001, B19.

Stepanchuck, S. & Wong, C. (1991) Mooncakes and Hungry Ghosts: Festivals of China. San Francisco: China Books & Periodicals.

Tan, A. (2000) Joy Luck Club. NY: McGraw-Hill College.

Tseng, W-S., & Hsu, J. (1972) The Chinese Attitude toward Parental Authority as expressed in Chinese Children's Stories. Archives of General Psychiatry, 20, 28-34.

Yu, L. (1974a) Chinese Women in History and Legend: Volume 1. New York: A.R.T.S., Inc.

Yu, L. (1974b) Chinese Women in History and Legend: Volume 2. New York: A.R.T.S. Inc.

ABOUT THE AUTHOR

Jean Lau Chin, Ed.D., ABPP is a psychologist and Professor at Adelphi University in New York. She has held senior management positions as academic Dean at two universities, Executive Director of a community health center, and Director of a mental health clinic. Her work on leadership, diversity, Asian American and women's issues include: Fulbright Scholar as Distinguished Chair in Cultural Competence, author of 12 books, numerous publications, and talks. She has served in many leadership positions on national, state and local boards promoting national policy on mental health, substance abuse, access to care, cultural competence, and women's issues. Most recently, she is Chair of the Council Leadership Team of the American Psychological Association, president of the International Council of Psychologists, and chairperson of the board of the Organization of Chinese Americans-Long Island. She was the first Asian American to be licensed as a psychologist in Massachusetts. She grew up in New York City's Chinatown during the 1940s-1960s, and has been a major contributor to the New York City Chinatown Oral History Project

9 781979 373234